"The Abencerraje" AND "Ozmín and Daraja"

"The Abencerraje" and "Ozmín and Daraja"

TWO SIXTEENTH-CENTURY NOVELLAS FROM SPAIN

EDITED AND TRANSLATED BY

Barbara Fuchs, Larissa Brewer-García,

and Aaron J. Ilika

PENN

University of Pennsylvania Press

Philadelphia

Published by

University of Pennsylvania Press

Philadelphia, Pennsylvania 19104-4112

www.upenn.edu/pennpress

Printed in the United States of America on acid-free paper

1 3 5 7 9 8 6 4 2

Library of Congress Cataloging-in-Publication Data

Abencerraje. English

"The Abencerraje"; and "Ozmín and Daraja" : two sixteenth-century
novellas from Spain / edited and translated by Barbara Fuchs, Larissa
Brewer-García, and Aaron J. Ilika. — 1st ed.

p. cm.

Includes bibliographical references.

ISBN 978-0-8122-4608-7 (hardcover : alk. paper)

1. Abencerraje. 2. Ozmín y Daraja. 3. Novelle—History
and criticism. 4. Romances, Spanish—History and criticism.
5. Romances, Spanish—Translations into English. 6. Muslims—
Spain—History—Sources. 7. Muslims in literature. I. Fuchs,
Barbara. II. Brewer-García, Larissa. III. Ilika, Aaron. IV. Ozmín y
Daraja. English. V. Title. VI. Title: Ozmín and Daraja.

PQ6271.A2E5 2014

863'.309—dc23

2013041217

Contents

711	Muslim troops cross the Strait of Gibraltar and defeat Visigoth troops at the battle of Guadalete.
711–714	Most of the Iberian Peninsula surrenders to Muslim forces.
711–756	Muslim rule of the Iberian Peninsula is controlled by the Caliph of Damascus.
756–1031	An independent Andalusian Umayyad Emirate reigns over the Iberian Peninsula.
1031	The Almoravids take over the Umayyad Caliphate of Córdoba.
1085	Christian King Alfonso VI of León and Castile captures Toledo.
1174	The Almohads take over the Almoravid reign.
1212	Christian forces defeat Almohad forces at the Battle of Las Navas de Tolosa.
1232	The Nasrid dynasty takes over Almohad territories.
1236	Christians capture Córdoba.
1238	Granada becomes the capital of the Nasrid kingdom.
1248	Christians conquer Seville.
1410	Christians seize Antequera.
1462	Christians conquer Gibraltar.
1469	Isabella I of Castile and Ferdinand II of Aragon are married, uniting Spain.
1481	King Muley Hacén (Abū al-Hasan ʿAlī) refuses to pay the annual tribute to the Catholic Monarchs and seizes the Christian city of Zahara.
1482	Christian campaigns against Granada begin.
1482–1492	Internecine battles among the Nasrid rulers weaken Muslim efforts to fight against Christian attacks. The major factions of the civil conflict are King Muley Hacén (and his brother Mohammed al-Zagal) and Muley Hacén's son

Mohammed XII (Abū 'Abd Allah), known as the Small King, or Boabdil.

1482   Leadership of Muslim territories in Andalusia is divided: Muley Hacén reigns from the city of Málaga with the support of his brother. Boabdil reigns from Granada with the support of the Abencerrajes.

1483   Ferdinand II captures Boabdil. In his absence, his father, Muley Hacén, wins back control of Granada. Ferdinand II releases Boabdil under the condition that he fight against Muley Hacén.

1484   *The plot of "The Abencerraje" begins some time after the Christian capture of Álora in June 1484.*

1485   Muley Hacén becomes ill and is deposed. His brother Mohammed al-Zagal takes over his reign. Muley Hacén dies.

1486   Boabdil fights against Mohammed al-Zagal in Granada but eventually accepts al-Zagal's rule. Shortly thereafter, Boabdil is captured again by Christian forces in battle. When he is released, he returns to fighting against al-Zagal in Granada.

1487   Boabdil takes over rule of Granada, occupying the Alhambra. Al-Zagal retreats to Guadix.

1488   Christians seize Málaga.

1489   Of the four territories that remain in Nasrid control, Boabdil controls Granada and al-Zagal controls Guadix, Baza, and Almería.

1489   Baza surrenders to the Christians.

1489   *The plot of "Ozmín and Daraja" begins.*

1489   In December, al-Zagal turns over his remaining territories (Guadix and Almería) to the Catholic Monarchs and emigrates to Northern Africa.

1492   Boabdil's official surrender to the Christians marks the end of Muslim political power on the Iberian Peninsula. Muslims living in Granada become subjects of Christian rule. The terms of surrender promise that the Muslims of Granada will be allowed to preserve their religion and culture.

1492   The Jews are expelled from Spain.

1492   Columbus arrives in the New World.

1499   The Muslim uprising in Granada is quickly quelled by the Crown.

1500–1502   The Crown pursues forced mass conversions of Muslims in Castile.

1511   The Crown prohibits converted Muslims, called Moriscos, in Granada from wearing Moorish dress.

1515–1516   Forced mass conversions of Muslims take place in Navarre.

1523–1526   Forced mass conversions of Muslims take place in Aragon.

1525   All Muslims are expelled from Aragon.

1526   The Edict of Granada prohibits the use of Moorish names, circumcision, non-Christian notaries, the bearing of arms by Moriscos, and Morisco meat vendors.

1526   The Morisco community of Granada pays Charles V to revoke the Edict of Granada. The edict is temporarily suspended.

1530   The Crown issues a decree requiring converted Muslims to wear "Christian" clothes.

1532   The Crown issues a decree against Morisco dances and songs that mention Mohammed.

1560–1561   The Crown's prohibition of silk exports and a tax on Granadan silk hurts many Moriscos' livelihoods.

1561   "The Abencerraje" is published as "Parte de la corónica del ínclito infante don Fernando, que ganó a Antequera" and also as an interpolated tale in a new edition of Jorge Montemayor's *Diana*.

1565   "The Abencerraje" reappears as part of Antonio Villegas's literary miscellany, the *Inventario*.

1565   Three spies of the Castilian Crown infiltrate a Morisco community in Segovia. They announce to the Crown that the Morisco community supports an alleged plan by Ottoman forces in Northern Africa to attack Spain.

1566	Philip II issues royal decrees to prohibit Moorish dress; Moorish celebrations, dances, and music; and the use of Arabic in spoken or textual communication.
1568–1570	In response to the repressive decrees, the Moriscos revolt in the mountains of the Alpujarras, near Granada, leading to a prolonged armed conflict.
1571	After defeating the Morisco uprising in the Alpujarras, Philip II disperses the Moriscos of Granada throughout other regions of the peninsula.
1571	The Holy League, a coalition of Catholic forces, wins the Battle of Lepanto, in present-day western Greece. This naval victory against Ottoman forces prevents the northern expansion of the Ottoman Empire.
1595	Ginés Pérez de Hita publishes the first part of his *Civil Wars of Granada*.
1596	Lope de Vega writes his play *El remedio en la desdicha*, based on "The Abencerraje" (pub. 1620).
1599	Mateo Alemán publishes "Ozmín and Daraja" as an embedded novella in the picaresque *Guzmán de Alfarache*.
1605	Miguel de Cervantes publishes part I of *Don Quixote*. Cervantes's first narrator finds the continuation of the story written in Arabic by the "Arab historian" Cide Hamete Benengeli and hires a Morisco who knows Arabic to translate it.
1609–1614	The Crown orders the forced expulsion of all Moriscos from the Iberian Peninsula.
1615	Miguel de Cervantes publishes part II of *Don Quixote*, which includes the sympathetic portrayal of Moriscos forced to leave Spain.

Widely read across Europe ever since their first publication, the anonymous "The Abencerraje" (1561) and "Ozmín and Daraja," from Mateo Alemán's *Guzmán de Alfarache* (1599), represent the epitome of Spain's literary idealization of Muslims. Finely wrought literary artifacts, both novellas reflect the intense engagement of early modern Spain with the cultural inheritance of Al-Andalus and offer rich imaginings of life on the Christian-Muslim frontier in what was until 1492 the Nasrid kingdom of Granada.[1] "The Abencerraje" depicts the friendship between two knights, a Moor and his Christian captor, while "Ozmín and Daraja" traces the adventures of two Moorish lovers during the war on Granada. Central examples of the tradition of literary maurophilia—the idealization of Moors in chivalric and romance texts— these stories reveal a profound fascination with a culture that was officially denounced. By recalling the intimate and sympathetic bonds that often connected Christians to the heritage of Al-Andalus in Spain, they offer a more nuanced view of the Christian-Muslim divide in the early modern period.

⊞ Maurophilia and the Moors in Spain ⊞

The two texts translated here are part of a varied and fascinating literary tradition that idealized the traditional enemies of Christian Europe—the Moors, or Saracens, as they were known in other contexts. While there are medieval examples of this tradition, it was especially rich in sixteenth-century Spain, particularly because it often contrasted markedly with official policies of discrimination and persecution against Muslims and their descendants. Although maurophilia trades in a series of recognizable topoi—heroic Moorish knights and their beautiful ladies, a courtly setting of elaborate entertainments and chivalric displays—it also emphasizes the place of the Moors in Spain.

Muslims had lived in Iberia since the Berber invasions of 711, set-
tling in most of the peninsula. Over the centuries, the various Christian rulers of Iberia gradually expanded their control, portraying the
conquest of territory from the Muslims as a *reconquista,* or *reconquest.*
This powerful coinage, still used in some quarters today, underscored
the Christians' supposed right to the territory and the inevitability
of their advance. In fact, during these centuries there were many versions of coexistence between Muslims, Christians, and Jews in Iberia,
from occasional moments of the idealized *convivencia* (coexistence)
imagined by the influential critic Américo Castro to the more frequent arrangements of *conveniencia* (convenience) noted by historian
Brian Catlos. Christian rulers and military leaders frequently established allegiances with the various Muslim kingdoms to further their
goals, and the three faiths lived together in a variety of formal and
informal arrangements, which generally involved paying a special tax
in exchange for religious freedom. Although these arrangements bore
little resemblance to modern notions of tolerance and were frequently
interrupted by violent episodes of religious persecution, the plurality
of religious and cultural forms in medieval Spain made for a rich and
rare culture. Life on the frontier between Christian and Muslim territories often involved small-scale conflict, including skirmishes such
as the one that leads to the capture of the Moor in "The Abencerraje."
These border raids sought booty and captives who would be ransomed
for money.

During the long centuries of the Muslim presence in Iberia, much
of the peninsula's aristocratic culture and its sense of courtly virtue
came from the kingdoms of Al-Andalus. Christians greatly admired
the elaborate Andalusi architecture, gardens, poetry, horsemanship,
furnishings, and fashions they found when they conquered such
important cities as Toledo (1085) and Seville (1248), and they soon
incorporated them as their own, creating a Castilian culture with
many shared elements (Dodds, Menocal, and Balbale 2008, 4): hence
the magnificent palace of the Alcázar in Seville, which Pedro I of Castile took over from his Muslim predecessors and greatly expanded.
Modeled on the great palace of the Alhambra in Granada, the Christians' palace is virtually indistinguishable from a "Moorish" building.

Whatever their own religion or ethnicity, the artisans who crafted it worked within a local idiom and produced Andalusi architecture, with its decorative tiles, elaborate wood carvings on the ceilings, delicate columns and patios, and so forth.

Over the centuries, this intense engagement with Andalusi forms hybridized Spanish culture to the extent that the "Moorish" origins of many architectural forms, costumes, and even styles of horseback riding were largely ignored; these were instead simply considered Spanish forms. There is a certain irony, therefore, when the fictional Queen Isabella encourages her captive, Daraja, to dress in the Castilian style: inventories inform us that the historical Isabella's wardrobe was full of "Moorish" wear, from her platform shoes to her *tocas de camino* (head wraps for travel). The change of dress she proposes to Daraja assumes a clearly marked difference far from the fusion of costumes evident in the period.

This broad cultural exchange and hybridization—in some cases deliberate and conscious, in others simply habitual—is a crucial context for the literary idealization of the Moor (Fuchs 2009). While the maurophile novellas may be idealizing in their focus on chivalry and exalted feeling, they also chart the vivid presence of the Andalusi heritage in quotidian Spanish culture. Beyond showcasing this shared material culture, moreover, the texts respond to specific political and cultural changes over the course of the sixteenth century, making a strong case for a sympathetic approach to Muslims and their Christianized descendants.

By the late fifteenth century, the Christians controlled all of modern-day Spain except the Nasrid kingdom of Granada. Ferdinand II of Aragon and Isabella I of Castile, known as the Catholic Monarchs, pursued this final goal, in no small part to solidify their own legitimacy as rulers over a newly unified Spain. In a series of campaigns over ten years (1482–1492), they gradually advanced on Granada. The fall of the Nasrid kingdom was accelerated by a series of internecine rivalries among the ruling families and leading clans, such as the fictional Moor Abindarráez describes when he relates the tragic history of the Abencerrajes to his Christian captor. These rivalries were chronicled in Ginés Pérez de Hita's maurophile *Guerras civiles de Granada* (Civil

Wars of Granada) (1595), a historical romance that relates the fall of the city amid a wealth of entertainments, love affairs, and the ballads that commemorate them. The two novellas translated here, though written in the mid- and late sixteenth century, are set in the years of these final campaigns: "El Abencerraje" occurs sometime after the capture of Álora, in 1482 (although there are some internal contradictions in its chronology, as we note below), while "Ozmín and Daraja" takes place in the final years of the war, from the surrender of Baza in 1489 to the fall of Granada itself in January 1492.

When Granada surrendered, the Catholic Monarchs offered terms that would have been recognizable to any medieval ruler of Iberia: in exchange for military and political submission, the Muslims of Granada would be allowed to preserve their religion and culture, simply changing political masters. The treaty even protected recent converts to Islam, allowing them to retain their chosen faith (Harvey 2005, 27). But this initial similarity to earlier peace treaties and accommodations proved illusory. Emboldened by this last step in the consolidation of Spanish territory and eager to promote Christianity as Spain's exclusive identity, the Catholic Monarchs (who had also, in 1492, decreed the expulsion from Spain of any Jew who would not convert to Christianity) soon began a policy of discrimination against Muslims and of forced conversions. Exasperated by the Christians' failure to respect the terms of the Capitulations, the Muslims of Granada rebelled against the authorities. As a revered Islamic scholar of the time put it, "If the King of the Conquest does not keep faith, what are we to expect from his successors?" (Yuce Banegas, quoted in Harvey 1990, 339). The Crown then used the rebellion to justify forcing Muslims not only in Granada but throughout Castile to convert or face exile (Harvey 2005, 21–22).

By the turn of the sixteenth century, the Crown of Castile was pursuing the mass baptism of its Muslim subjects. A royal decree of 1502 formalized the requirement compelling all inhabitants of its territories to become Christians, thereby erasing legal guarantees that were in some cases centuries old. While some religious authorities argued for an incremental and syncretic approach to conversion, including the use of Arabic to proselytize, they were quickly overruled by those who favored a more belligerent approach. Thus, many of the Moriscos, as these forcibly converted Muslims were known, became Christians with very little understanding of their new religion or, indeed, much say in the matter. At the same time, the Crown began to pass laws against various forms of Moorish dress and other cultural practices, even beyond what was strictly religious. Yet for the most part, the Moriscos were able to delay the implementation of such laws with a series of generous gifts to the Crown.

Meanwhile, the Crown of Aragon (Catalonia, Aragon, and Valencia), which included many more Muslims who had long lived under Christian rule than those in Castile, gradually moved toward enforced conversion. Although Ferdinand resisted applying Castilian policies to his kingdom, Charles V, who ruled over all of Spain, soon expanded the forced conversions to Aragon. Charles swiftly broke his initial promise not to force conversion on his Muslim subjects, and in 1525, an edict was passed decreeing the expulsion of all Muslims from the Crown of Aragon. The point of this edict was by no means to expel the Muslim population but rather to force them to convert (Harvey 2005, 94). In effect, it drove much Muslim worship underground.

For decades, Spain lived in an uneasy equilibrium with its formerly Muslim subjects: by the late 1520s, they all were nominally converted, and basically tolerated, though possibly few believed in the authenticity of a Christianity that had been imposed on them. In fact, some Moriscos, particularly among the elites, soon assimilated seamlessly into Christian society, while others were clearly crypto-Muslims, and there existed a series of syncretic practices between these two ends of the spectrum. Many regions of Spain, including Valencia and Andalusia, had large Morisco populations that continued to be central to the local economies, particularly as they cultivated the great estates of the nobility.

The general situation for all converts to Christianity deteriorated markedly as the Crown sought to identify and police religious divergence. In a Counter-Reformation context in which the fear of Protestantism and other heresies was widespread, the authenticity of converts' belief became a constant source of concern. Even after the Crown had compelled Jews and Muslims to convert and the Inquisition had persecuted any visible straying from approved religious practice, they could not compel faith or belief. As Deborah Root has argued, the indeterminability of faith may have led to a new definition of authentic Christianity based on genealogy. By this definition, "New" Christians, whether *conversos*—former Jews and their descendants—or Moriscos—former Muslims and their descendants—could never be "truly" Christian because of their ancestry (Root 1988, 130). Religious difference was thus transformed into a genealogical taint located in the blood and construed similarly to some modern notions of racial difference, while the ethnic difference of *conversos* and Moriscos was assumed to reflect their religious intractability.

This new and profoundly suspicious attitude toward New Christians was compounded over the course of the sixteenth century by a series of laws that restricted the opportunities available to them and demanded *limpieza de sangre* (purity of blood) in order to enter certain universities and religious orders, to emigrate to the New World, or to access a number of privileges across the social and political sphere. Many voices across society challenged the statutes, and the hypocrisy of compelling Jews and Muslims—not to speak of the huge indigenous populations of the New World—to convert while withholding from them the full privileges of being an "Old" Christian did not go unnoticed. In his 1606 treatise on the Moriscos, the humanist chronicler Pedro de Valencia argued for "a total mix, in which it is impossible to discern or distinguish which is of this or that nation," and recommended also that "those who gradually are born to marriages of Old Christians and Moriscos should not be treated as or held as Moriscos, and neither the ones nor the others should be offended or despised" (Valencia 1997, 136–37).

The possibility of actually making the distinctions required by the purity of blood laws depended on individuals somehow being legible and transparent—as though past religious affiliations really did manifest physically. But there was no visible difference among these people, many of whom had intermarried for centuries and whose families had converted long ago. Religious identity was never crystal clear, and the higher the stakes, the more likely dissimulation became. In this context, literary representations of characters who passed, deliberately impersonating other identities, became part of the ongoing debates about tolerance and assimilation, underscoring the impossibility of ever firmly distinguishing among subjects (Fuchs 2003, 3). Thus, as we discuss below, the dazzling series of identities adopted by the protean hero of "Ozmín and Daraja" makes him impossible to classify or restrain.

Beyond the challenge posed by the purity of blood statutes, the uneasy equilibrium in which Moriscos had existed for decades was challenged when the Crown finally decided to implement the repressive legislation against their culture, passed in some cases decades earlier. The laws forbade "Moorish" garments, music, and celebrations, as well as, crucially, the use of Arabic. The proposed enforcement led in 1568 to a widespread uprising in Granada, known as the War of the Alpujarras (a remote mountain range near Granada where the rebels took refuge). The uprising took the Crown by surprise and proved very difficult to quell: it raged for over two years, and entire towns were laid to waste when they offered resistance. The consequences of the uprising were utterly devastating for the Moriscos: many were enslaved as war booty, and the rest were exiled from Granada and resettled elsewhere in Spain.

By the end of the sixteenth century, when Alemán published *Guzmán de Alfarache*, the Moriscos had suffered through decades of cultural repression, internal exile, and persecution. Yet Alemán portrays a world only one hundred years earlier in which both Ozmín and Daraja are admired and desired. The constant foregrounding of the attraction that Moors hold—for Christians as for other Moors—is one of the signal ideological interventions of this maurophile text and particularly striking in contrast to the heightened anti-Morisco rhetoric of the late sixteenth century.

By the 1580s, the Crown had become convinced of the Moriscos' supposed intractable difference and was seeking a final solution to the problem they ostensibly posed as internal others. Anti-Morisco pamphlets anathemized them as a bad seed, a race that represented the stubborn root of evil within Spain, in a heated rhetoric that denied them even the most basic humanity. Conveniently, getting rid of the Moriscos would also cancel any debts owed to them and make their property available to Old Christians. Some counselors suggested deporting the Moriscos to Africa, but others worried that they would only attack

Spain from there. Wild schemes were floated to settle the Moriscos on the coasts of Newfoundland and to castrate them so that they might not reproduce (Harvey 2005, 294-97). Although Spain had expelled its Jews in 1492, these unprecedented proposals were now being made as a way to deal with converted Christians, however nominal their belief may have been. (As we have noted, Moriscos ran the gamut from crypto-Muslims to fully assimilated Christians, but the proposals made no such distinctions.) By the turn of the seventeenth century, a policy of expulsion seems to have been agreed on, and all that remained was to work out the details. From 1609 to 1614, a series of decrees compelled the expulsion of the Moriscos under pain of death. This time, no conversion could ensure their place in Spain: indeed, many of the families expelled had been at least nominally Christian for over a century.

The extraordinary fate of Muslims and Moriscos in the loaded century between the fall of Granada and the final expulsions makes maurophilia a particularly trenchant genre. Far from fanciful or fashionable confections, as some early critics held, maurophile texts advance a powerful argument for the place of the Moors and their descendants within Spain (Fuchs 2009). From the striking interfaith friendship in "The Abencerraje" to the irresistible Muslim lovers of "Ozmín and Daraja," these texts legitimize "the Moor" and implicitly link their sympathetic protagonists—all of whom, we are told, have a long line of descendants— to the Moriscos that readers might have encountered in their own time.

In wide circulation across Europe from the early modern period on, these texts contributed to the development of European Orientalism, while indelibly linking Spain to its Moorish inheritance. While they may have helped popularize the notion of an exotic Spain abroad, however, within Spain they played a very different role, insisting on the quotidian reality of Moors and Moorishness and on their indisputable place in the Spanish imaginary as in its society.

▨ "The Abencerraje" ▨

The anonymous novella "The Abencerraje" tells of a Moorish knight, Abindarráez, of the unfortunate clan of the Abencerrajes. After his noble family is decimated in internecine palace struggles in the city of Granada, Abindarráez is brought up in exile by the governor of Cártama. He falls in love with the governor's daughter and his supposed sister, Jarifa. Once they discover, to their great relief, that they are not actually related, they decide to marry in secret. The text opens with Abindarráez on his way to meet Jarifa, a journey interrupted by Rodrigo de Narváez, governor of the frontier town of Álora, and his Christian knights. In a skirmish, Abindarráez fights them valiantly but is nonetheless defeated and taken captive. When Narváez learns of his captive's interrupted nuptials, however, he frees him on Abindarráez's solemn word as a knight that he will return to his captivity. Abindarráez journeys on, consummates his secret union with Jarifa, and only then explains his vow to her. She insists on accompanying him back to captivity, expressing her surprise at the strong bond between the two men. Narváez welcomes them generously and, in a show of great magnanimity, decides to let Abindarráez and his bride go free, refusing to accept any ransom for them.

The novella was first published in 1561 and exists in at least three slightly different versions. The anonymous edition of 1561 presents itself as a fragment of a historical narrative, under the title *Parte de la crónica del ínclito infante don Fernando, que ganó a Antequera* [Part of the Chronicle of the Famous Prince Don Ferdinand, Who Conquered Antequera]. Critics have not reached any definite conclusions about the novella's authorship, even though its two subsequent versions appear within authored works: although it was not part of the original publication of the wildly popular pastoral *Diana*, by Jorge de Montemayor (1559), it was included as an interpolated tale in the 1561–62 edition of the text, as well as in its many subsequent editions and translations across Europe. It also appeared as one of the items in Antonio Villegas's literary miscellany, the *Inventario*, of 1565. Both of these authors are generally presumed to have been *conversos*, who often voiced some of the most powerful veiled criticisms of Spanish orthodoxy in their literary production. Critics have speculated that the generous depiction of the Moors and of Christian-Muslim friendship in "The Abencerraje" made it a powerful and controversial text in a time of increasing official repression of the nominally converted Moriscos—hence the anonymity of the original version. Yet the popularity of the novella was such that it was subsequently included in authored texts, essentially authorizing it and hugely expanding its readership.

Soledad Carrasco Urgoiti convincingly argues that "The Abencerraje" expresses the political and economic preference for tolerance of a particular class—the landed aristocracy of Aragon, which employed many Moriscos as agricultural workers and had no wish to see them persecuted by a centralized monarchy of which it was deeply suspicious. The anonymous *Corónica* version includes a striking dedication to Jerónimo Jiménez de Embún, an Aragonese nobleman who participated in the local resistance to the persecution of Morisco vassals by the Inquisition and other agents of the centralized state (Carrasco Urgoiti 1972).

Beyond this specific address, the novella offers a powerful vision of friendship between Christians and Moors. Israel Burshatin has argued that the Christian, Narváez, always has the upper hand in the text, from his initial defeat of Abindarráez to his ability to decide on the fate of the lovers (Burshatin 1984, 197). While "The Abencerraje" may not portray the absolute parity of Moors and Christians, however, it emphasizes that their friendship as chivalric equals is both rare and worthy. The bond between the knights begs the question of what collective ties might follow from the individual allegiances chronicled in the text.

The novella appears particularly interested in questions of memory and memorialization. This was a freighted issue in sixteenth-century Spain: how, after the fall of Granada, were the Moors to be remembered? What was to be their place—and that of their descendants—in the now stridently Christian nation? "The Abencerraje" subtly addresses these questions. The opening and closing paragraphs of the more sophisticated *Inventario* version, on which our translation is based, link the individual connection between Narváez and the Moor to broader historical concerns, emphasizing the importance of fame and historical memory.

The Christian hero Narváez, governor of Antequera and Álora, is literally larger than life. A historical figure by that name participated in the conquest of Antequera in 1410 and became governor of the town; he died some years later, in 1424. He cannot thus be the Narváez who governed the second town, Álora, taken by the Christians only in 1482. The conflation of at least two separate historical figures in one character, "famous for his virtue and feats of arms," suggests that the text engages with Spain's recent history at an allegorical rather than a documentary level. It also signals a concern with the broad progress of the war on Granada rather than with any specific encounter, so that the plot takes on an almost metonymic quality.

Nonetheless, the text insists from the very start on the importance of fame and commemoration. No sooner is Narváez named than we are told that "he fought the Moors with great valor, and especially in the campaign and the battle for Antequera he performed deeds worthy of eternal memory, were it not that our Spain takes such skill for granted. For it is so natural to Spain and so common here that anything one does seems too little; unlike for the Greeks and Romans, who in their writings turned men who once risked death into immortals and set them amongst the stars." The reader might reasonably expect that this narrative, with its praise of Narváez's virtue, will fill the gap left when Spain takes its heroes for granted, providing the missing story of war and conquest. Yet instead of supplementing the absence of epic, the narrative takes a very different turn, moving quickly from the epic and historical mode of the introduction and the initial encounter between Abindarráez and his Christian captors to chivalric romance, a mode more appropriate for narrating the friendship between the noble protagonists and the love story of Abindarráez and his beloved. Given the delicacy of the exchanges between captor and captive and Narváez's generosity to the Moor, the frontier becomes a space of friendship rather than the front line of a protracted conflict.

This romance refiguration is expressed in the intense ties that bind the two men. The analogy between Abindarráez's erotic captivity—a Petrarchan conceit—and his actual confinement is an organizing principle of the novella. Abindarráez curtails Narváez's power over him, explaining that he has been defeated by another: "You may well kill me," said the Moor, "for I am in your hands, but I cannot be conquered except by the one who once conquered me." Yet the remarkable closeness that develops between the two men makes the metaphor reversible: if love is like captivity, then captivity is a little like love. Abindarráez's vow to return to Narváez both recalls the earlier promises exchanged by the lovers and anticipates the secret marriage, binding the two knights as closely as Abindarráez is bound to Jarifa.

When Abindarráez returns with his bride in order to keep his promise, Narváez expresses his concern for Abindarráez's wounds, which Jarifa had somehow missed as she and her lover consummated their union. Jarifa is profoundly unsettled at the realization that a greater intimacy—the symbolically laden wounds in the thigh and the arm— binds the two men. It is important to recover the intensity of this homosocial relationship in order to appreciate how fully "The Abencerraje" reimagines Moorish-Christian relations. The chivalric bond transcends the heterosexual union between Abindarráez and Jarifa, and replaces the more common fiction of exogamous romance—the love of a Christian man for a Moorish woman—through which Moorish-Christian relations were often managed in cultural fantasy.

The text's closing emphasis on posterity returns us to the crucial questions of how this notable friendship will be remembered. In a letter to Jarifa thanking her for the rich gifts that she and Abindarráez have sent him, Narváez reiterates how monumental his own actions seem to him, once again emphasizing the national over the individual: "Fair Jarifa: Abindarráez has not allowed me to enjoy the real triumph of his captivity, which consists in forgiving and doing good, and since never was a mission offered me in this land so noble or worthy of a Spanish captain, I would like to enjoy it fully and to craft a statue of it for my posterity and descendants." With this gesture of commemoration, Narváez's feat of generosity becomes exemplary. By presenting the governor as a model subject, worthy—at least in his own eyes—of a national monument and national fame, "The Abencerraje" offers itself as a monument to coexistence and amity. And whereas Narváez, in the text, does not actually have any descendants, the text imagines for itself a reading audience that will treasure and commemorate its central gesture of friendship. History may recall Narváez as a conqueror of Antequera, but the statue that he longs to erect and the literary monument that actually immortalizes him both focus on his generosity to a Moor. "The Abencerraje" thus supplies a different kind of history, one in which religious difference and political allegiance matter much less than nobility and individual friendship.

Unlike many of the maurophile texts that follow, "The Abencerraje" makes virtually no mention of religion. The differing faiths are primarily invoked, in fact, to note that they make no difference to the friendship between Narváez and the Moors, when Jarifa's father urges Abindarráez and Jarifa to send the knight a generous gift and "keep him henceforth as a friend, even though we are of different faiths." Conversely, many of the subsequent maurophile fictions, including "Ozmín and Daraja," place their sympathetic Moorish characters on some kind of path toward Christianity, whether because they have secretly always wished to be Christians, because they suddenly see the light, or, more cynically, because conversion seems the politic approach to the situation that they face. "The Abencerraje" is striking for its sympathy for Moors qua Moors, with no intimation whatsoever that these are Christians in the making or future converts. Of course, these Moors are literary constructs who cite Greek myths and communicate easily with Christians, but their very depiction makes a point about their familiarity.

"The Abencerraje" was hugely influential both within Spain and beyond. In countless ballads, the story of the lovers Abindarráez and Jarifa was repeated across Spain. Included within the sensationally popular pastoral romance *Diana* (1562), the novella was read and translated wherever that best-seller went. Its central topoi—aristocratic and chivalric courtliness, material opulence, beleaguered love in the context of war—were picked up by Pérez de Hita for his historical romance, *Civil Wars of Granada*. So popular was the figure of the Moorish knight that when Cervantes's famous would-be knight, Don Quixote (1605), lies wounded after his first sortie, he imagines himself as Abindarráez, confounding the neighbor who tries to assist him:

> One cannot help but think that the devil made Don Quixote recall stories suited to the events that had occurred, because at that point, forgetting about [the chivalric knight of ballad tradition] Valdovinos, he remembered the Moor Abindarráez, when the governor of Antequera, Rodrigo de Narváez, captured him

and brought him back to his domain as a prisoner. So when
the farmer asked him again how he felt and what was wrong,
he answered with the same words and phrases that the captive
scion of the Abencerraje family said to Rodrigo de Narváez, just
as he had read them in the history of *Diana*, by Jorge de Montemayor, where they are written, and he did this so deliberately
that as the farmer walked along he despaired at hearing such
an enormous amount of foolishness. (Cervantes 2003, 42–43)

The appeal of Abindarráez trumps the Moor's traditional role as the
enemy of the chivalric knight, leading Don Quixote to identify with
him instead. Don Quixote (and presumably Cervantes) thinks of "The
Abencerraje" in the context of the pastoral *Diana*, one of the few books
saved from Don Quixote's library when it is consigned to the flames.
It represents for him a comfortingly familiar literary idealization,
shared by the pastoral, the "Moorish," and the chivalric romance, as
so many delectable flavors of a favorite treat. Yet for Cervantes's novel
as a whole, this fleeting romance identification has important consequences. It reminds us that despite its protagonist's strong misgivings
at his own story being narrated by an "Arab historian" (the second
narrator, Cide Hamete Benengeli), he identifies more easily with the
Moorish hero of "The Abencerraje" than with its Christian, chivalric
protagonist. This brief passage thus provides strong evidence of how
the maurophile novella tempered anti-Muslim and anti-Morisco prej-
udice, if only on the page.

   "The Abencerraje" was widely disseminated in the early modern
period. By the middle of the seventeenth century, over twenty-four
editions had been published as part of Montemayor's *Diana* in cities
throughout Spain, Flanders, Italy, and Portugal. During this period,
also as part of Montemayor's *Diana*, at least twelve editions of at least
two different French translations, six editions of two different German translations, and six editions of Bartholomew Yong's English
translation were published. Even beyond the sixteenth and seventeenth centuries, "The Abencerraje" continued to be a seminal story
for conceptions of "the Moor" across Europe, as well as for Romantic
orientalism, including Washington Irving's *Tales of the Alhambra* and

François-René de Chateaubriand's *Le dernier Abéncerage*. As its broad and enthusiastic reception across the centuries signals, the text's vision of a chivalric friendship that transcends religious difference holds an enduring appeal.

⊠ "Ozmín and Daraja" ⊠

"Ozmín and Daraja" looks back to "The Abencerraje" for the idealization of the Moors and for its chivalric milieu, but its later date makes its positive portrait of the Moors, whom Spain had increasingly persecuted and marginalized over the course of the sixteenth century, much more striking. As we noted above, by the 1590s many in Spain had given up on the possibility of ever assimilating the Moriscos into Spanish society, and there was already significant discussion of banishing them from the country. By reprising the positive portrayal of "The Abencerraje," therefore, "Ozmín and Daraja" makes a striking pro-Morisco intervention into the debates.

The story follows the pair of lovers after Daraja falls captive to the Catholic Monarchs, Ferdinand and Isabella, at the taking of Baza during the war on Granada, shortly before the Christian triumph in 1492. The location is significant: Baza was the area with the most voluntary conversions to Christianity in the late fifteenth century and saw particularly close relations between local elites and the Christian conquerors. Daraja's bilingualism and the resulting difficulty in categorizing her are established immediately: "She spoke Spanish so well that it would have been difficult to tell that she was not an Old Christian, for as a fluent speaker she could pass for one." Although the novella is set much earlier, Daraja's linguistic passing corresponds closely to the linguistic assimilation of many Moriscos by the late sixteenth century, and her ability to negotiate Christian culture more generally proves crucial to the story.

While Daraja languishes as a pampered prisoner in the house of a Christian noble, the desperate Ozmín takes on a variety of disguises in order to reach his beloved, from a lowly gardener to a Christian knight. Both he and Daraja succeed in manipulating the affections of the Christians: while Daraja plays one suitor off the other, Ozmín befriends them and impresses everyone with his dexterity in bull-fighting, horsemanship, and jousting. The lovers' story is ultimately resolved only through the intervention of the monarchs, who convert the couple to Christianity and enable their marriage. Given the many instances of deception throughout the story, however, the conversion seems like just one more instance of the protagonists' resourcefulness when facing overwhelming opposition. So although it may seem that the sympathetic representation of Moors in the text depends on their progress toward Christianity, that final goal is obliquely questioned and challenged by the constant duplicitousness into which the characters are forced.

This later example of the maurophile novella thus echoes the humanist emphasis in "The Abencerraje" on tolerance and amity across confessional divides but adds a baroque twist in the protean transformations and strategic opacity of its protagonists. It also signals the genre's engagement with the political realities of the late sixteenth century, in that even its most sympathetic Moors must be brought into the Christian fold by the narrative's end. If "The Abencerraje" inaugurates the maurophile genre, then, "Ozmín and Daraja" takes it to its most elaborate, and politically urgent, form.

Although entirely set in southern Spain, the novella has strong echoes of Heliodorus's far-ranging ancient romance, the *Aethiopica*, or, as it was sometimes known, *The Loves of Theagenes and Clariclea*. This Byzantine romance had grown wildly popular in Spain from the moment it was rediscovered and translated from the Greek, with seven editions between 1554 and 1616. Alemán's tale echoes several of *Aethiopica*'s main elements: two sympathetic lovers separated by the heroine's captivity, an emphasis on their sexual purity, even as they resort to all kinds of deceit and dissimulation in order to be reunited, and even a scene in which one of the lovers is asked to serve as a pander for the other (McGrady 1966, 50–51). These traces of the Byzantine romance conjure sympathy for the lovers as a couple, foregrounding their fully reciprocated passion rather than exoticizing the female Moorish beloved as is so often the case in the ballad tradition.

The place of "Ozmín and Daraja" within *Guzmán de Alfarache* also suggests intriguing connections between the maurophile novella and the popular picaresque. If "The Abencerraje" was a fitting addition to the idealized world of the pastoral *Diana,* the far more cynical and knowing "Ozmín and Daraja" finds its place within a picaresque universe. Although, of necessity, we have translated only the maurophile tale here, it is important to note the many rich connections with its picaresque context. Mateo Alemán's *Guzmán de Alfarache* is the cynical, first-person story of a *pícaro* (rascal) coming of age and of his many unsavory adventures. Repentant and reformed, he tells his story, ostensibly as a cautionary tale. Critics have long debated the authenticity of Guzmán's reformation and the reliability of his first-person narrative voice. Alemán himself led a colorful life, which provided ample material for his description of marginality in the novel. He was born and lived much of his life in Seville, where "Ozmín and Daraja" is set. He was often taunted as *Poca Sangre,* or "little blood," for his possible *converso* origins (Alemán 1997, 15). Always short of funds and picking quarrels with the powerful, he was constantly in trouble with the law, even while serving the Crown as an accountant and a judge.

Within *Guzmán de Alfarache,* the story of Ozmín and Daraja is related to the young *pícaro* and his companions by a priest in order to pass the time as they travel between Seville and the neighboring town of Cazalla. Although the tale, with its incomparable and noble protagonists, certainly reflects the idealizing tradition of maurophilia, it also betrays certain picaresque affinities. Ozmín's serial disguises, episodic adventures, and menial positions cannot help but recall those of a *pícaro,* and both he and Daraja ably trick their masters—whether employers or captors—in order to achieve their own goals. If the idealizing novella is tarnished by these traces of the picaresque, the picaresque is also enriched by these clearly positive instances of resourcefulness and self-fashioning: both texts notably foreground characters' reinvention of themselves and their abandonment of their origins. Perhaps the greatest constant between the interpolated tale and its frame is the unreliability of compelled speech—as also, we might add, of compelled belief or morality. What can one actually believe of what Ozmín and Daraja say to the Christians who surround them, given how little leeway for expression, much less for action, they enjoy? And how does their tactical, strategic relation to the truth throughout the novella overshadow their conversion at the end? The problem of unreliability and interestedness is foregrounded in the succinct account that the narrator, Guzmán, gives us after the priest's story is over: "We had listened to that story in complete silence for the whole way, until we arrived within view of Cazalla. He seemed to have timed it perfectly, even though he told it to us at greater length and with a different soul than I have recounted it here."

Within the novella itself, words often mean very different things to different listeners, and the reader is forced to confront this relativism. When Ozmín needs to communicate with Daraja in her friend Doña Elvira's hearing, he sings an Arabic song, as Doña Elvira scornfully dismisses the "savage" who "hums nonsense." When the noble Don Rodrigo entreats Ozmín, who is disguised as a gardener, to persuade Daraja to convert so that he, an Old Christian, can marry her, Ozmín's equivocal answer suggests the relativism of religious fervor: "The same reason with which you seek to bind me, Don Rodrigo, will make you believe how much I long for Daraja to follow my faith, as I have countless, multiple times persuaded her. My own wish in this matter is none other than your own." The priest who is narrating the story emphasizes the equivocation, lest the reader miss it: "The Moor had not lied at all in what he said, had his true meaning been understood." Religious difference is thus both marked and relativized by the exchange: everyone is equally attached to his or her religion, at least until the end of the story.

If religious difference is carefully negotiated, cultural difference tends to disappear in the aristocratic Seville of the text. The story features as local color many of the entertainments that Pérez de Hita and the Moorish ballads had made so central to maurophilia. There are many pages devoted to the splendor and excitement of bullfights and especially the games of canes, in which quadrilles of lavishly costumed riders executed a set of maneuvers on horseback while throwing light reeds at each other. Yet the bullfights and the equestrian games are here Christian affairs, their Moorish origins largely unremarked. Daraja provides the occasion for the festivities, which are an attempt to cheer her up, but no Moors officially participate. The single exception is Ozmín, who covers his face and pretends to be a foreigner. For Alemán, exquisite horsemanship is a local trait: the riders on their *jineta* saddles—an Andalusi heritage—seem one with the horse, he claims, "For in most of Andalusia—in Seville, Córdoba, Jerez de la Frontera—children are placed—so they say—from the cradle onto the saddle, just as in other places they are given hobbyhorses to ride." Local style has so fully absorbed the Andalusi heritage that Christians practice "Moorish" forms without particularly remarking upon them (Fuchs 2009).

Amid shared cultural practices, the narrative underscores the protagonists' ability to negotiate the two camps. The disguised Ozmín is sought out by Don Alonso, another Christian suitor for Daraja's hand, in order to challenge Don Rodrigo. Ozmín proceeds to tutor Don Alonso not in the Moorish equestrian games, as one might expect, but in jousting. His double expertise—and particularly his striking ability on horseback "on both saddles"—finally lead Alonso to doubt Ozmín's assumed identity as a laborer.

As these aristocratic rapprochements suggest, class trumps religion as the significant divide in the world of the text, echoing "The Abencerraje." Noble Moors are as heroic and ideal as Christians, if not more so, and Daraja is constantly desired by the Christian nobles, even though she ends up with her rightful spouse. Despite the constant suggestion of threatening suitors, the greatest threat to the couple's happiness comes from an unruly mob of yokels, who do not play according to any rules that Ozmín can figure out. And despite the fact that the lovers spend almost the entire story forced to equivocate about their true identity and beliefs, their final conversion—no questions asked—grants them inclusion in the Christian polity, projected into the future via their "illustrious lineage." Ozmín and Daraja's origins never get in the way; no one in this world worries about purity of blood, although they are quite exercised about class. Moreover, both Christians and Moors share a culture so thoroughly marked by Andalusi forms that any acculturation is relative. For these noble Moors, at least, there is nothing foreign about Spanish culture (Fuchs 2009).

The tale of Ozmín and Daraja is particularly unorthodox and ideologically slippery because of its belatedness. If the 1561 "Abencerraje" ended with the conversion of Abindarráez and Jarifa, it would not hold for us the same interest as a powerfully ambiguous maurophile text. But by the time Alemán wrote his story, the legal repression of the Moriscos, the uprising in the Alpujarras, the forced resettlements, and the increasing calls for a definitive solution to the Morisco "problem" had fundamentally changed the situation. Only in this radicalized context could the conversion of the protagonists and their virtually forced abandonment of their religion be read as a sympathetic resolution. Ozmín and Daraja represent that first, presumably most reluctant, generation of Moriscos; their idealization, their desirability, and, most important, their cultural compatibility with the Christians who surround them offer up the possibility of full assimilation for their descendants. This inclusive stance toward Moorish origins offers a brave alternative, however compromised, to the contemporary arguments against supposedly unassimilable and recalcitrant Moriscos, even if some of the ethnic animus against them is redirected against the lower classes.

Like "The Abencerraje," "Ozmín and Daraja" was widely read in its original and in translation in early modern Europe. Before the end of the seventeenth century, as part of *Guzmán de Alfarache*, the story of the two Moorish lovers was published at least twenty different times in its original, eighteen different times in French, twelve different times in English, nine different times in German, five different times in Dutch, and five different times in Italian. It was also translated into Latin. In its wide dissemination, it offered an idealized vision of assimilable and hugely sympathetic Moors, intimately connected to Spain and eminently deserving of their place within it, while nonetheless recalling the strategic dissimulation into which repression had forced their descendants, the Moriscos, in the fraught century of their forced conversions.

▦ Our Translations ▦

We have based our translations on standard critical editions of the texts: Francisco López Estrada's edition of "El Abencerraje (Novela y romancero)," first published in 1980, and José María Micó's edition of Alemán's *Guzmán de Alfarache*, originally published in 1997. López Estrada's edition is based on the *Inventario* edition of the novella in 1565, arguably the most careful and complete one, and also the only one that includes a prologue. Micó bases his work on the last edition of

Guzmán that Alemán himself corrected: Seville (1602), in a copy from the Bibliothèque Nationale in Paris, with occasional corrections based on the princeps (Madrid, 1599). Since we are dealing with regularized and critically edited texts, we have not faced significant problems of variant readings.

We have also consulted Bartholomew Yong's early modern translation of "The Abencerraje" in his *Diana of George of Montemayor* (1598) and James Mabbe's translation of "Ozmín and Daraja" in *The Rogue*, as his 1622 version of *Guzmán de Alfarache* was known. Both of these translations were produced in a world where chivalry and jousts were still familiar, and their chosen registers offer important insights into the texts' imaginary. Mabbe (or "Don Diego Puede-Ser," as he punningly referred to himself in the prologue to *The Rogue*) was an expert translator who also tackled Cervantes and other writers. Unlike Yong, who takes significant liberties with the text, Mabbe goes out of his way to capture details and hew close to the original; his translation is both inspired and inspiring.

Contextual Materials

This volume offers a number of materials that serve to contextualize the two novellas. Besides a comprehensive historical-literary chronology and a bibliography, we include examples of maurophile literature influenced by or related to the novellas: a sample of popular ballads and an excerpt of Ginés Pérez de Hita's *Civil Wars of Granada*. We also offer an overview of legislation and other official documents on the Moriscos, tracing the arc of their official repression from the fall of Granada to their expulsion in 1609–14, and an excerpt of the well-known petition by the Morisco advocate Francisco Núñez Muley against the repressive legislation.

A Note on Coinage

Three different kinds of coins are mentioned in the novellas: the Zahene gold piece, the doubloon, and the double doubloon. All three were made of high-quality gold. The Zahene gold piece, referenced in "The Abencerraje," was a Moorish coin still used during the time of Ferdinand and Isabella. The doubloon and the double doubloon that appear in "Ozmín and Daraja" are Spanish gold coins printed with a coat of arms. Doubloons had a coat of arms on each side, whereas double doubloons had two coats of arms on each side and were worth twice a normal doubloon (Vigo 1997, 36).

Here we have calculated their approximate worth at the times the novellas were first published, yet it is important to note that by the sixteenth century, gold coins were rarely used as currency but rather considered precious objects whose value exceeded an exchange value. Elvira Vilches (2013) explains this unique value of gold coins by the late sixteenth century with the following example: "Already in 1567 Tomás de Mercado [in *Suma de tratos y contratos*] explained that *doblones*, a piece of 2 escudos, were outstanding coins whose bright golden glitter he compared with that of a fine pearl or precious stone. He also noticed that the beauty and greatness of *doblones* make them suitable for royalty and the aristocracy because they rarely were minted and thus were held as precious objects of exceptional value" ("Coins, Value, and Trust," 103). Thus, the gold coins cited in theses novellas, like their Moorish protagonists, were relatively obsolete but still treasured for their "exotic" value and aristocratic charm.

Zahene gold piece = a gold coin worth 425 *maravedís*.[2]

Doubloon = a gold coin worth 850 *maravedís*.

Double doubloon = a gold coin with four coats of arms, worth 1,700 *maravedís*.

NOTES

1 Throughout this introduction, we alternate the more precise terms "Muslim" and "Andalusi-derived" with the all-purpose "Moor" and "Moorish," since the latter two more closely approximate the term *moro*, widely used in the period, and also capture the ambiguous connection between "Moorish" subjects and the Muslim religion, the various polities of Al-Andalus, and an increasingly marginalized "race" of Moriscos over the course of the sixteenth century. All translations are ours unless otherwise noted.

2 The *maravedí* (after 1497) was not a coin but rather a monetary unit of measurement. In 1550, a laborer earned approximately 40 *maravedís* a day, and by the end

of the sixteenth century, he or she would earn 85 *maravedís* a day (Nalle 1999, 131). In this context, the sums of 6,000 *doblas zaenes* (2,550,000 *maravedís*) and 1,000 *doblados* (1,700,000 *maravedís*), cited respectively as ransom amounts in "The Abencerraje" and "Ozmín and Daraja," exceed what average day laborers could have made in an entire lifetime.

Part I
The Novellas

---------------------◼ "The Abencerraje" ◼---------------------

Prologue

This is a living portrait of virtue, generosity, valor, nobility, and loyalty, composed of Rodrigo de Narváez[1] and the Abencerraje and Jarifa,[2] as well as her father and the king of Granada. Although the two make up the body of this work, the others adorn the canvas and have left their own marks on it. And just as a precious diamond, whether set in gold or silver or lead, retains its fair value according to its carats and its luster, so too virtue shines and shows its qualities in any flawed subject, just like the seed that grows when it falls on fertile soil and in the barren soil is lost.[3]

◼ "The Abencerraje" ◼

The story goes that in the time of Prince Ferdinand, who conquered Antequera, there was a knight named Rodrigo de Narváez, famous for his virtue and feats of arms. He fought the Moors with great valor, and especially in the campaign and the battle for Antequera he performed deeds worthy of eternal memory, were it not that our Spain takes such skill for granted. For it is so natural to Spain and so common here that anything one does seems too little; unlike for the Greeks and Romans, who in their writings turned men who once risked death

---

[1] Rodrigo de Narváez was the name of a historical person who participated in the Christian conquest of Antequera in 1410 and was named its governor by Prince Ferdinand of Antequera.

[2] In Arabic, Abindarráez (the first name of the Abencerraje) means "captain's son," and Jarifa means "noble, precious, or beautiful one." The Abencerraje family was a noble clan in Al-Andalus.

[3] In the biblical parable (Matthew 13:3–23; Mark 4:3–20; Luke 8:5-8), Christ compares spreading his word to the sowing of seeds: just as soils may be fertile or barren, some people will be more receptive to the spreading of the Word than others.

into immortals and set them among the stars. This knight, then, did so much in the service of his king and his faith that after the town was conquered he was named governor, so that having played such a great role in taking it, he would now do the same in defending it. He was also made governor of Álora, and so commanded both garrisons, dividing his time between the two and always attending to the greater need. He was usually to be found in Álora, where he had fifty noble squires in the king's service for the defense and safety of the town. And none was ever found lacking, for, like the immortal knights of King Darius, whenever one died, they set another in his place. They all had such great faith in their captain's virtue and took such strength from it that nothing was ever difficult for them: they never ceased to attack their enemies and defend themselves against them. They triumphed every time they skirmished, winning honor and profit, which enriched them always.

One night when the weather was very mild, the governor spoke these words to his squires after supper:

"It seems to me, noblemen, my brothers and lords, that nothing so rouses the hearts of men as the continual exercise of arms, through which we gain experience with our own weapons and lose fear of the enemy's. There is no need for me to invoke distant examples of this, as you yourselves are the best proof. I mention this because it has been many a day since we have done anything to increase our renown, and I would not be doing my duty to my office and my person if I let the time go to waste with such virtuous men and valiant troops at my command. It seems to me, if you are all in agreement, that with this clear and safe night beckoning to us, we should let our enemies know that the guardians of Álora do not sleep. That is my wish; do what you will."

They answered that he should lead and all would follow him. He chose nine of them and had them armed. Once ready, they left through a hidden door so that they would not be noticed and the fortress would remain safe. Setting out on their way, they came to a fork in the road, where the governor addressed them:

"If we all take one path, our prey might escape on the other. You five take this one, and I will take the other with these four. If by chance any of you find enemies that you cannot defeat, blow your horn, and the sound of it will call the others to your aid."

The five squires set out on their path, speaking of various things, when one of them said, "Hold on, friends, for unless I am mistaken, there is someone coming."

They hid in a thicket by the road and heard noises. Taking a closer look, they saw a gallant Moor coming toward them on a roan horse. He was of powerful build and had a beautiful face, and he looked very fine in the saddle. He wore a crimson cloak and a damask burnoose of the same color, all embroidered in gold and silver. His right sleeve was turned back, with a beautiful lady embroidered on it, and he held a fine and sturdy lance with two points. He carried a shield and a scimitar, and wore a Tunisian head wrap with many folds that served to both adorn and protect him.[4] So dressed, the Moor advanced with a noble air, singing a song he had composed in fond memory of his love, and which went like this: "Born in Granada, raised in Cártama, I fell in love in Coín, bordering Álora."

Although the music lacked artistry, the Moor did not lack for happiness, and his heart, which was full of love, gave charm to his every word. The squires, transported by the sight of him, almost let him through before they set upon him. Finding himself ambushed, he bravely came to his senses and waited to see what they would do.

Four of the five squires rode off to the side while one attacked him. But since the Moor was more skilled in those matters, with a stroke of his lance he forced the squire and his horse to the ground. Seeing this, three of the four remaining attacked him at the same time, for he seemed to them very strong. Now there were three Christians, any one of whom could take on ten Moors, against this one Moor, and yet all of them together could not defeat him. Soon the Moor found himself in great danger, as his lance broke and the squires pressed him hard. Feigning flight, he spurred his horse on with his legs and rushed toward the squire he had unhorsed. Like a bird he swooped from his

[4] As we note in the introduction, fine "Moorish" garments such as those worn here by Abindarráez would have been admired and worn not only by Muslims but also by Christians of the aristocratic classes.

saddle and grabbed the man's lance, and with it he turned upon the enemies who chased him as he pretended to flee. He fought so skillfully that in a short time he had two of the three on the ground. The last one, seeing his companions' dire need, sounded his horn as he rode to help them. Now the skirmish became very fierce, for they were affronted to have one knight last so long against them, while he fought for his life and more. Then one of the squires struck him on the thigh with his lance, in a blow so hard that, had it not landed askew, it would have gone right through him. Furious at finding himself wounded, the Moor turned and struck him with the lance, throwing both horse and rider to the ground, badly wounded.

Rodrigo de Narváez drew near, sensing that his companions needed help. As he rode the best horse, he took the lead. When he witnessed the Moor's bravery, he was astonished: the Moor had four of the five squires on the ground and the fifth one on the way.

"Moor, ride against me," he said, "and if you defeat me, I will vouch for the others." They joined in a bitter fight, but since the governor was fresh and the Moor and his horse were injured, Narváez pressed him so that he could not keep up. Yet seeing that his life and happiness hung on this one battle, the Moor threw such a blow at Narváez that it would no doubt have killed him, had he not stopped it with his shield. Parrying the blow, Narváez charged against him and wounded him on his right arm. Closing in, he grappled with him and threw him from his saddle to the ground. Then, leaning over him, he said, "Sir, concede defeat, or I shall kill you."

"You may well kill me," said the Moor, "for I am in your hands, but I cannot be vanquished except by the one who once vanquished me."

The governor did not remark on the mystery of these words; with his usual decency, he helped the Moor to his feet, for the wound that the squire had given him on his thigh and the other one on his arm (though not severe), coupled with his great exhaustion and the fall from his horse, had quite drained him. With supplies he took from the squires, Rodrigo bound up the Moor's wounds. Then he helped him onto one of the squires' horses, for his own was wounded, and they took the road back to Álora. While they all rode along, discussing the Moor's good bearing and bravery, he let out a great deep sigh and spoke a few words in Arabic that none of them could make out.[5] Observing the Moor's fine build and bearing, and recalling what he had seen him do, Rodrigo de Narváez suspected that such great sadness in such a brave heart could hardly come from what had just occurred.

To learn more, he said to him, "Sir, consider that the prisoner who loses all hope forfeits his right to liberty. Consider, too, that in war knights must both win and lose, for the better part of their battles are subject to fortune. For one who has just shown such valor, it seems like weakness to show so little now. If you sigh from the pain of your wounds, know that you are on your way to a place where you will soon be cured. If you lament your imprisonment, know that these are the ways of war, to which all who wage it are subject. And if you suffer some other secret torment, confide in me, for I promise you on my honor as a knight to do all in my power to remedy it."

The Moor, lifting his gaze from the ground, said, "What is your name, knight, you who show such understanding of my plight?"

He responded, "They call me Rodrigo de Narváez; I am the governor of Antequera and Álora."

The Moor, whose face brightened a bit at this, said, "Truly now some of my sorrow lifts, since though fortune was against me, it has left me in your hands. For although I have never seen you before, I have heard of your virtue and experienced your strength. So that you will not think that the pain from my wounds is what makes me sigh, and since it seems to me that you could keep any secret, send off your squires so that I may have two words with you."

The governor had them fall back. When they were alone, the Moor said to him with a great sigh:

"Rodrigo de Narváez, renowned governor of Álora, listen to what I shall tell you now, and you shall see whether my misfortunes are enough to break the heart of a captive man. They call me Abindarráez

---

[5] The original uses *entendió* (understood) instead of *entendía* (could understand) here: the squires may well have known Arabic but could not make out what Abindarráez mumbled. Christians on the frontier in Al-Andalus would have been likely to know Arabic. Cf. Abindarráez's love song earlier in the text, which the squires overhear, and the language of which is never specified.

the Younger, to distinguish me from an uncle of mine, my father's brother, of the same name. I come from the line of the Abencerrajes of Granada, of whom you must have often heard—although my present grief is quite enough, without recalling sorrows past, I want to tell you that story.

"In Granada there lived a line of noblemen called the Abencerrajes who were the finest in the kingdom: in their elegance, good grace, disposition, and bravery they excelled all others. They were favored by the king and all the nobles and well-loved by the common people. They emerged as victors from any combat they entered and distinguished themselves in all tournaments; they devised all the finery and costumes. So one could truly say that in times of peace as in war they were a model and example for the entire kingdom. It is said that there was never an Abencerraje who was miserly or cowardly or ill disposed. A man was not considered an Abencerraje if he did not serve a lady, nor was a woman considered a lady if she had no Abencerraje as a suitor.

"Yet fortune, their great enemy, decreed that they should fall from this excellence, as you will now hear. The King of Granada, led on by false information he had received against them, did a great wrong to two of these noblemen, the bravest of them all. And it was said, though I don't believe it, that these two and ten others at their request conspired to kill the King and divide the kingdom among themselves, avenging their insult. This conspiracy, whether true or false, was discovered, and so as not to scandalize the kingdom that loved them so, the King had them all beheaded in one night, for had he delayed his injustice, he would not have been able to carry it out. The King was offered huge ransoms for their lives, but he would not even hear of it. When the people saw that there was no hope for their lives, they began to lament anew. The fathers who had sired them wept, as did the mothers who had given birth to them; the ladies whom they served wept, as did the knights who were their companions. The common people raised such a great and lasting outcry it was as though enemies had invaded the city. If their lives could have been bought with tears, the Abencerrajes would not have died so miserably.

"Behold what became of such a distinguished lineage and its famous knights! Consider how long it takes for Fortune to raise a man and how quickly she cuts him down; how long it takes for a tree to grow and how quickly it goes to the fire; how difficult it is to build a house and how rapidly it burns! How many could learn from those wretched men, who blamelessly suffered their public disgrace! Even though they were so numerous and so important and had enjoyed the favor of the King himself, their houses were destroyed, their estates given to others, and their name proclaimed treasonous throughout the kingdom. Because of this unfortunate episode, no Abencerraje was allowed to live in Granada, except for my father and uncle, who were found innocent of this crime, on the condition that any sons born to them be raised outside the city, never to return, and any daughters married outside the kingdom."

Rodrigo de Narváez, who observed the suffering with which the Abencerraje related his misfortunes, said to him:

"Yours is certainly a strange story, sir, and a great injustice was done to the Abencerrajes, for it is hard to believe that men such as they could have committed treason."

"It is just as I have told you," answered the Abencerraje, "Wait and you shall hear how, from that time on, all the Abencerrajes were unfortunate. When I came into the world from my mother's womb, my father sent me to the governor of Cártama, his close friend, in order to fulfill the king's decree. The governor had a daughter about my age, whom he loved more than himself, for not only was she his only child and most beautiful, but she had cost him his wife, who had died giving birth to her. She and I were as brother and sister in our childhood because that is what we heard people call us. I cannot recall a moment when we were not together. We were raised together, walked together, ate and drank together. From this closeness came a natural affection that increased with age. I remember that one afternoon when I walked into the place they call the Garden of Jasmine, I found her seated by the fountain, arranging her lovely hair. I gazed at her, vanquished by her beauty, and she seemed to me like Salmacis.[6] I said to myself, 'O to

---

[6] In the Greek myth retold by Ovid in book four of the *Metamorphoses*, Salmacis falls in love with Hermaphroditus (son of Hermes and Aphrodite) when he is bathing by a fountain. When he rejects her, she asks the gods to combine their bodies into one.

be Hermaphroditus and appear before this beautiful goddess!' How I regretted that she was my sister! Yet I rushed to her, and when she saw me, she hurried to meet me with arms outstretched. Seating me by her side, she said to me,

'Brother, why did you leave me alone for so long?'

'My lady,' I replied, 'I have been searching for you for a long time, and no one could say where you were, until my heart told me. But tell me now, how certain are you that we are brother and sister?'

'I only know it from the great love I have for you, and from the fact that everyone calls us that,' she said.

'And if we were not,' said I, 'would you love me as much?'

'Can you not see,' she said, 'that if we were not, my father would never let us spend so much time alone together?'

'Well, if it would mean the loss of that good fortune,' I said, 'I would rather have my present sorrow.'

Then she began to blush, and said, 'What do you lose from our being brother and sister?'

'I lose myself and you,' I said.

'I don't understand you,' she said. 'In fact, it seems to me that simply being brother and sister naturally compels us to love one another.'

'Only your beauty compels me. The kinship actually seems to discourage me sometimes.'

"Lowering my eyes in embarrassment at what I had said, I saw her exact likeness in the waters of the fountain. Wherever I turned my head, I saw her image, and most of all in my heart. I said to myself (for I would not have wanted anyone to hear me), 'If I were to drown myself in the fountain where I see my lady, I would have a better excuse than Narcissus![7] If she loved me as I love her, how happy I would be! And if fortune allowed us to live together always, what a life I could lead!'

"Saying this, I stood up and gathered some of the jasmine that surrounded the fountain, threading it with myrtle to make a beautiful garland. Placing it on my head, I turned to her, both crowned and vanquished. She looked at me, more sweetly it seemed than usual, took the

---

[7] In the myth retold in book three of Ovid's *Metamorphoses*, the beautiful Narcissus falls in love with his image reflected in a stream, falls in while gazing at himself, and drowns.

garland from me and placed it on her head. At that moment she seemed to me more beautiful than Venus when she was judged for the apple.[8] Turning to me, she asked, 'How do I look now, Abindarráez?'

'As though you have just vanquished the world and they are crowning you its queen and lady,' I answered. She stood up and took me by the hand, saying, 'If that were the case, brother, you would lose nothing by it.' I did not answer and instead followed her out of the garden. We led this life of dissimulation for a long time, until Love took revenge on us and exposed the ruse, for as we grew older, we both learned that we were not siblings. I know not what she felt when she first found out, but nothing has ever made me happier, although I have paid dearly for it since. No sooner were we certain of this, but the pure and healthy love we had for each other began to spoil, turning into a raging malady that will last until our deaths. Here there were no first causes to excuse because our love came from a pleasure and delight that was nothing but good. Yet the harm did not come at first, but suddenly and all at once: I now found all my joy in her, and my soul followed the measure of her soul. What I did not see in her seemed to me ugly, unnecessary, and of no use in the world; all my thoughts were with her. By this point, our pastimes had changed: I now looked at her in fear of being found out and was jealous of the very sun that touched her. Her presence wounded me, and her absence broke my heart. And yet for all this, she did not owe me anything because she paid me in the same coin. Then Fortune, jealous of our sweet life, decided to snatch away our happiness, as you shall hear.

"The king of Granada, wishing to promote the governor of Cártama, ordered him to leave his garrison for Coín, which is that town near yours, and to leave me in Cártama under the new governor. Imagine, if you have ever been in love, how my lady and I felt when we learned this disastrous news. We met in a secret place to weep at our parting. I called out to her, 'My lady, my soul, my only happiness,' and other names love had taught me. 'When your beauty is far away from me, will you ever remember this captive of yours?' Here my tears and

---

[8] When Venus, Juno, and Minerva competed for a golden apple promised to the fairest goddess, Paris of Troy awarded Venus the prize.

sighs cut short my words. Forcing myself to continue, I half muttered some confused notions that I cannot even remember because my lady took my memory with her. Who could relate how she lamented, although it still seemed too little to me! She said a thousand sweet words to me that I can hear even now. Finally, so that no one would hear us, we said good-bye with many tears and sobs, and with a sigh wrenched from our souls, we gave each other an embrace as a pledge of our love.

"Then, because she saw me in such straits, looking as though I would die, she said, 'Abindarráez, leaving you is breaking my heart, and since I know you feel the same, I want to be yours until death. My heart is yours, my life is yours, my honor and wealth. As proof of this, as soon as I find a way to meet you while my father is indisposed or away, which I eagerly await, I will send word to you from Coín, where I now go with him. Come to me wherever I am, and there I shall give you, as my husband, that which I carry with me, for neither your loyalty nor my nature would allow it otherwise, and everything else has been yours for many years.'

"With this promise my heart calmed down somewhat, and I kissed her hands for the favor she promised me. They left the next day, and I was left as one who, walking through steep and rugged mountains, loses sight of the sun. I began to feel her absence sharply and sought false cures for it. I gazed at the windows where she used to sit, the waters where she bathed, the room where she slept, the garden where she rested. I visited all her stations,[9] and in all of them I found an image of my suffering. The hope she had given me that she would summon me sustained me, and so I fooled my cares somewhat. Sometimes the delay caused me even greater pain, so that I would have preferred for her to leave me in despair, which causes pain only until it is believed certain, while hope troubles us until desire is fulfilled.

"My good fortune had it so that this morning my lady fulfilled her promise to me and sent one of her trusted servants to summon me. Her father had left for Granada, called for by the King to return immedi-

---

[9] Abindarráez visits the places where Jarifa used to be with the reverence of a worshipper viewing representations of Christ at the stations of the cross.

ately. Revived by this good news, I readied myself. I waited for nightfall
so as to leave in secret, and put on the garments in which you found me
to show my lady the joy in my heart. I would not have thought that a
hundred knights at once would have been enough to stop me since I
carried my lady on my sleeve. If you defeated me, it was not by force,
which is not possible, but rather because my bad luck or heaven's will
snatched away my good fortune. So consider now, at the end of my
story, the good I have lost and the misfortune that weighs on me. I was
traveling from Cártama to Coín—a short trip, although desire made
it longer—the proudest Abencerraje ever: I went at the behest of my
lady, to see my lady, to love my lady, and to marry my lady. Now I find
myself wounded, captive and defeated, and the worst part is that the
short space of my good fortune ends this evening. Allow me to find
consolation in my sighs, Christian, and consider them not weakness,
for it would take even greater fortune to be able to suffer such desperate straits."

Rodrigo de Narváez was amazed and touched by the Moor's
strange affair, and since it seemed to him that nothing could harm his
purpose more than delay, said to him:

"Abindarráez, I want to show you that my virtue is stronger than
your ill fortune. If you give me your word as a knight to return as my
captive in three days' time, I will set you free to go on your way, since I
would be sorry to prevent such an affair."

The Moor was so happy when he heard this that he tried to throw
himself at Narváez's feet, saying, "Rodrigo de Narváez, if you do this,
you will have done the greatest kindness that man ever did, and you
would give me new life. As for what you ask of me, take whatever assur-
ance you will, for I shall fulfill it."

The governor called his squires and said, "My lords, entrust this
prisoner to me, for I will guarantee his ransom." They told him to command as he pleased. Taking the Moor's right hand between his own, he
said, "Do you swear to me as a knight to return to my castle in Álora to
be my prisoner within three days?

He said, "I swear."

"Then good luck, and if you should need me or anything else for
your enterprise, it shall be done as well."

Abindarráez thanked him and set off in haste for Coín. Rodrigo de Narváez and his squires returned to Álora, discussing the bravery and fine bearing of the Moor.

In his hurry, Abindarráez pressed on and did not take long to reach Coín, heading straight for the castle. He did not stop until he found a door, as he had been instructed. Pausing there, he began his reconnaissance to see if there was any need to defend himself. Seeing that all was well, he knocked on the door with the back of his lance, for this was the signal that the lady-in-waiting had given him. She quickly opened the door herself and said to him, "What has taken you so long, my lord? Your delay had us greatly worried. My lady has long awaited you; dismount, and you shall go to her."

He dismounted and placed his horse in a well-hidden spot nearby. He left his lance with his shield and scimitar, and then the lady-in-waiting led him by the hand as quietly as possible so that the people of the castle would not hear him. They climbed a staircase and reached the bedchamber of the lovely Jarifa, for this was the lady's name. She had already heard him and came out to welcome him with outstretched arms. In their great joy, they embraced without a word.

Then the lady said, "What has taken you so long, my lord? Your delay has caused me great sadness and alarm."

"My lady," he said, "you know full well it could not have been my negligence, but things do not always turn out the way we wish."

She took him by the hand and led him to a secret chamber. Sitting on a bed that was there, she said, "Abindarráez, I long to show you how the captives of love keep their promises, for from the day I gave you my heart as a token, I have been trying to win it back. I ordered you to come to this castle to be my prisoner, as I am yours, and, as my husband, to make you the owner of my person and of my father's estate, even though I suspect that shall go against his wishes. He does not know your bravery, nor has he experienced your virtue as I have, and he would like to give me a richer husband. But I take your person and my happiness to be the greatest treasure in the world."

And saying this, she hung her head, ashamed to have revealed so much. The Moor took her in his arms, kissing her hands many times for the favor she granted him, and said, "My lady, in exchange for all the good you have offered me, I have nothing to offer you that is not yours already, save this token as a sign that I take you as my lady and wife."

After summoning the lady-in-waiting, they spoke their marriage vows. Now, being married, they lay in their bed, where the new experience stoked the fire in their hearts. In this conquest, many loving words and actions were exchanged, which are better imagined than written.

Afterward, the Moor became lost in thought and, distracted, let out a great sigh. The lady, unable to suffer such a slight to her beauty and devotion, lovingly brought him back to his senses and asked, "What is this, Abindarráez? It seems that my happiness brings you sorrow. I hear you sigh and twist and turn all around. If I am your all and your happiness as you told me, for whom do you sigh? And if I am not, why did you deceive me? If you have found some fault with my body, look upon my devotion, which should be enough to outweigh many faults. If you serve another lady, tell me who she is so that I may serve her too. If you have another secret sorrow that will not offend me, tell me, for I will either free you from it or die in the attempt."

The Abencerraje, embarrassed by what he had done and believing that if he did not confess he would provoke great suspicion, told her with an impassioned sigh, "My lady, if I did not love you more than myself, I would not have complained. I suffered my grief bravely when it was just my own, but now that it forces me to leave you, I have no strength to bear it. Know that my sighs come from too much fidelity rather than the lack of it. I want to tell you what has happened, so you will not wonder."

Then he told her everything that had occurred and at the end said, "So, my lady, your captive is also the governor of Álora's. I do not fear the sorrow of imprisonment for you taught my heart to endure, but living without you would be death itself."

The lady smiled and told him, "Do not worry, Abindarráez. I shall take care of your ransom for it is my duty. I hold that any knight who gives his word to return to prison keeps it as long as he sends whatever ransom is asked of him. And so name the sum you see fit, for I have the keys to my father's treasure and will give them to you so that you can send of it what you will. Rodrigo de Narváez is a praiseworthy knight. He gave you your liberty once when you entrusted this matter to him, and this now obliges him to be even more virtuous. I think he will be satisfied, since if he had you in his power, he would only ask for the same."

The Abencerraje replied, "My lady, your great love for me prevents you from counseling me wisely; I shall certainly not commit such a great fault. If I was obliged to keep my word when I came on my own behalf to see you, now that I am yours, my obligation has redoubled. I shall return to Álora and place myself in the governor's hands; after I do what I must, let him do as he pleases."

"May God never allow you to go into captivity while I go free, for I would not be so," Jarifa said. "I wish to accompany you on this journey, for neither my love for you nor my fear of my father, having offended him, will allow me any choice in the matter."

The Moor, weeping tears of happiness, embraced her and said, "My lady, you are always granting favors upon favors; do as you please for that is what I want."

Having come to this agreement, they gathered provisions and set out the next morning. The lady covered her face so as not to be recognized.

As they were on their way, discussing various things, they came across an old man. The lady asked him where he was going, and he answered, "I'm going to Álora for I have some business with the governor, who is the most virtuous and honorable knight I have ever known."

Jarifa was pleased to hear this, for it seemed to her that if everyone found so much virtue in this knight, they, who were in so much need of it, would find it also. Turning to the traveler, she said, "Tell me, brother, do you know of any memorable deed this knight has done?"

"I know many," he said, "but I can tell you one that will stand in for all the rest. This knight was first the governor of Antequera, where for a long time he was in love with a beautiful lady. He performed a thousand courtesies in her service, too many to relate. Yet even though she knew the worth of this knight, she paid him little attention because she loved her husband so much.

"It happened that one summer day, having finished dinner, she and her husband went down to an orchard in their estate. He carried a sparrowhawk on his hand and slipped it at some birds, which fled and hid in the brambles. The wise hawk, holding its body back, reached in with its talons and killed many of them. The knight fed it and, turning to the lady, said, 'What do you think, my lady, of how cleverly the hawk trapped the birds and then killed them? I'll have you know that when the governor of Antequera skirmishes with Moors, he pursues them and kills them like that.' She asked who the governor was, pretending not to know him. 'He's the bravest and most virtuous knight I've ever seen.' He began to speak of him very highly, so that the lady felt a certain regret and said to herself, 'Well! Men are in love with this knight, and I am not, though he is in love with me? Surely I shall be forgiven for whatever I do for him, since my own husband has told me how deserving he is.'

"The next day it happened that the husband was away from the city and the lady could resist no longer, so she had a servant send for the knight. Narváez was nearly beside himself with joy, although he could hardly believe it, recalling the harshness she had always shown him. Yet he still went discreetly to see her at the appointed time. She waited for him in a hidden place, and there she realized the great wrong she had committed and the shame in seeking one who had sought her for so long. Her thoughts turned to Fame, who reveals all things; she feared the fickleness of men and the offense to her husband. All these obstacles served only to vanquish her even further, as is usually the case. Ignoring them all, she received him sweetly and ushered him into her bedchamber, where they exchanged many kind words. At last she said, 'Lord Rodrigo de Narváez, I am yours from this day forward, as is everything in my power. Do not thank me, for all your passions and entreaties, whether true or false, had no effect on me. Rather, thank my husband, who told me such things about you that they have put me in this state.' Then she told him about the conversation with her husband and concluded, 'In fact, my lord, you owe more to my husband than he owes you.'

"These words struck Narváez, causing him worry and remorse for the wrong he was committing against one who had so praised him. He stepped away, and said, 'In truth, my lady, I love you full well and shall love you always, but God forbid that I should commit such a cruel offense against one who has spoken of me so highly. Instead, from this day forward, I shall safeguard your husband's honor as though it were my own, for that is the best way to repay him for the good things he has said of me.' And without further ado, he left the way he came. The lady must have felt duped, yet the knight no doubt acted with great virtue and bravery, my lords, for he overcame his own desire."

The Abencerraje and his lady were amazed at the story. He praised Narváez greatly, saying that he had never seen greater virtue in a man. She replied, "By God, my lord, I would not wish for such a virtuous servant. He must not have been too much in love since he left so quickly and the husband's honor moved him more than the lady's beauty." And she said a few other clever things about the matter.

Just then they arrived at the fortress. They knocked at the gate, and it was opened by guards who already knew what had happened. One man ran to summon the governor, saying, "My lord, the Moor you defeated is here in the castle, and he has brought a noble lady with him."

The governor suspected who it was and came downstairs. The Abencerraje, taking his bride by the hand, approached him and said:

"Rodrigo de Narváez, see whether I have kept my word, for I promised one prisoner and I bring you two, one of whom would suffice to vanquish many others. Behold my lady; consider if I have suffered rightly. Take us as your own, for I trust you with my lady and my honor."

Narváez was delighted to see them and said to the lady, "I know not which of you owes more to the other, but I am in great debt to you both. Come in, and take your ease in this your house; consider it as such from now on, for its owner is your servant."

With that they went to the rooms that had been prepared for them, and soon after they ate something, for they were weary from their journey. "How are your wounds, sir?" the governor asked Abindarráez.

"It seems that with the journey they are inflamed and somewhat sore, sir."

The lovely Jarifa became upset: "What is this, my lord? You have wounds of which I know nothing?"

"My lady, whoever survives the wounds that you give thinks little of any others. It is true that the skirmish the other night left me with a few scrapes, and the journey and not tending to them must have done me some harm."

"It would be best," the governor said, "for you to lie down, and a surgeon from the castle will attend you."

Immediately the lovely Jarifa began to undress him in great dismay. When the doctor came and examined him, he said it was nothing and applied an ointment to relieve the pain. In three days' time, he was cured.

One day after dinner, the Abencerraje spoke these words: "Rodrigo de Narváez, since you are so wise, you may well surmise our situation from the manner in which we arrived. My hope is that you will be able to solve this unfortunate business. This lady is the beautiful Jarifa, of whom I spoke to you, my lady and my wife. She did not wish to remain in Coín for fear of having offended her father—she fears this even now. I know full well that the king loves you for your virtue, even though you are a Christian—I beg you to ask her father to pardon us for having done this without his knowledge, since Fortune brought it about in this way."

The governor said to them, "Take heart, for I promise you I shall do everything in my power." And taking ink and paper he wrote a letter to the King, which read thus:

▣ Letter from Rodrigo de Narváez, Governor of Álora, ▣ to the King of Granada

Most noble and powerful King of Granada:

Rodrigo de Narváez, Governor of Álora, your servant, kisses your royal hands and says: the Abencerraje Abindarráez the Younger, who was born in Granada and raised in Cártama under the authority of its Governor, fell in love with the beautiful Jarifa, his daughter. Later, you favored the Governor by transferring him to Coín. The lovers were secretly betrothed to confirm their love. When Abindarráez was summoned to the fortress due to the absence of Jarifa's father, whom you have with you, I happened across him on his way. After a skirmish I fought with him, in which he proved himself to be very valiant, I took him prisoner. When he told me his situation, I took pity on him and freed him for two days; he went to see his wife, so that on his journey he lost his freedom but won the lady. When she learned that the Abencerraje was returning to my captivity, she came with him and thus both of them are now in my power. I beg you not to let the name Abencerraje offend you, for I know that both this one and his father were not to blame in the conspiracy perpetrated against your royal person; they live as evidence of that. I entreat your Royal Highness to join me in assisting these unfortunate ones. I will pardon their ransom and will graciously release them, but only you can make her father pardon them and receive them in his good graces. And with this you will prove true to your greatness, proceeding as I would always expect of you.

When he had written the letter, he dispatched it with a squire, who gave it to the King as soon as he reached him. The King, knowing whose letter it was, was very pleased, for he loved this one Christian for his merits and good deeds. When he read it, he turned to the Governor of Coín, who was with him, and calling him aside, said:

"Read this letter from the Governor of Álora." When Jarifa's father read it he became very upset. The King said, "Do not be angry, even though you have good cause; know that there is nothing the Governor of Álora can ask me that I will not grant. And so I command that you go straight to Álora now to see him and to pardon your children and take them home. In return for this service, I will always favor them and you."

The Moor resented it in his heart, but seeing that he could not avoid the King's commandment, he put a good face on things and said he would do as his highness commanded.

He immediately left for Álora, where already they had heard from the squire what had happened and where everyone received him with great happiness and rejoicing. The Abencerraje and Jarifa came before him with great contrition and kissed his hands. He received them graciously and said:

"Let us not dwell on the past. I forgive you for having married without my consent, and as for the rest, my daughter, you chose a better husband than I could ever have given you."

Narváez held feasts in their honor for many days, and one night, after dining in a garden, he said, "I am so proud to have played a part in bringing this matter to a good end that nothing could make me happier. The only ransom I require, therefore, is the honor of having had you as my prisoners. From this day forth, lord Abindarráez, I free you to do as you wish."

They kissed his hands for the favor and kindness he had shown them, and the next morning they left the fortress with the Governor accompanying them partway.

Once they had arrived in Coín and were enjoying the good fortune they had so longed for, their father said to them, "My children, now that by my wish you control my estate, it would be right to show Rodrigo de Narváez the gratitude you owe him for the good deed he did you. He should not lose your ransom just because he was so generous; instead, he deserves a much larger one. I shall give you six thousand Zahene gold coins;[10] send them to him and keep him henceforth as a friend, even though we are of different faiths."

Abindarráez kissed his hands and received the doubloons. He sent them to the Governor of Álora, along with four beautiful horses and four lances with golden hilts and points, as well as four shields, and wrote him this letter:

▨ Letter from the Abencerraje Abindarráez ▨
to the Governor of Álora

If you think, Rodrigo de Narváez, that by freeing me in your castle so that I could return to mine you set me free, you deceive yourself, for when you freed my body, you captured my soul. Good works make prisoners of noble hearts. Where you are in

---

[10] The *zahén* was a valuable gold coin still used by Moors in the time of the Catholic Monarchs. Some claim it is named after Abū Zayān, king of Tlemcen (*Diccionario de la real academia española*), while others attribute it to Zaen, the thirteenth-century king of Valencia (Cantos Benítez 1763, 94). In the late sixteenth century, 6,000 Zahene gold pieces (approximately 2,550,000 *maravedís*) amounts to what an average laborer (who made approximately 85 *maravedís* a day) could only have made after 30,000 days of work. See the introductory Note on Coinage.

the habit of doing good to those you could destroy so as to gain honor and fame, I am obliged to thank you and serve you so as to follow my forebears and not sully the noble bloodline of the Abencerrajes but instead gather and distill in my veins all their blood that was shed. This small gift comes with the great love of the one who sends it, and that of Jarifa, which is so pure and loyal that it pleases me.

The Governor admired the worth and uniqueness of the gift, and accepting the horses, lances, and shields, he wrote this to Jarifa:

▣ Letter from the Governor of Álora ▣ to the Fair Jarifa

Fair Jarifa: Abindarráez has not allowed me to enjoy the real triumph of his captivity, which consists in forgiving and doing good. Since never was a mission offered me in this land so noble or worthy of a Spanish captain, I would like to enjoy it fully and to craft a statue of it for my posterity and descendants. I accept the horses and weapons to defend him from his enemies. And if by sending the coins, he proved himself a generous knight, by accepting them I would seem a greedy merchant. I grant them to you in payment for the favor you showed me by making use of me in my castle. Besides, my lady, I am not accustomed to robbing ladies, but rather to serving them and honoring them.

And with that he sent the doubloons back to them. Jarifa received them and said, "Whoever thinks to surpass Rodrigo de Narváez in combat or courtesy should think again." And so they remained very satisfied and pleased with each other, and linked by bonds of friendship so tight that they lasted a lifetime.

————————————— ✠ "Ozmín and Daraja" ✠ ———————————

MATEO ALEMÁN

Guzmán de Alfarache recounts the story of the two lovers Ozmín and
Daraja, as it was told to him.

As soon as they had finished praying, which was a very brief affair,
they closed their prayer books and placed them in their satchels. Everyone paid close attention as the good priest began the promised story.[1]

✠   ✠

The Catholic Monarchs Don Ferdinand and Doña Isabella had laid
siege to Baza,[2] a place so bitterly contested that for a long time neither
side had the advantage. Even though the army of their Royal Majesties
had great numbers, the Moors were also numerous and benefited from
the location of the town.

Queen Isabella was in Jaén arranging the necessary provisions,
while King Ferdinand personally attended to the army. He had
divided the force into two sections: on the one side the artillery was
entrusted to the Marquises of Cádiz and Aguilar, to Luis Fernández Portocarrero, lord of Palma, and to the knight commanders of
Alcántara and Calatrava, with other captains and soldiers; and on the
other lay his own camp with most of his knights and men, with the
besieged city between the two.[3]

---

[1] As we explain in the introduction, the novella appears in the first book of *Guzmán de Alfarache* (1599), a picaresque novel by Mateo Alemán. The larger story recounts the life of the poor
son of a Genoese *converso*, a descendant of converted Jews, who at the age of fourteen leaves
home to seek his fortune on the road. While Guzmán makes his way from Seville to Cazalla
with some travelers, a priest in their company narrates the tale of Ozmín and Daraja.

[2] The siege of Baza described here took place in 1489.

[3] Alcántara and Calatrava were military orders for knights in service of the Castilian Crown.
Some characters referred to in this account of the siege of Baza, such as King Ferdinand, Queen

Had the Christians been able to cut through the city, their two camps would have been a scant half league from each other. But since they could not pass, they went by way of the mountains, adding another half league, and so lay one league away from each other. Because it was difficult for the King's men to protect themselves, they decided to build trenches and fortifications, which the King often visited in person. Although the Moors tried to prevent their construction, the Christians defended the fortifications valiantly so that no day went by without two or more skirmishes, with many wounded and dead on each side. In order to keep the construction going, given its importance, companies of soldiers watched over the laborers night and day as necessary.

One day, when Don Rodrigo and Don Hurtado de Mendoza, governor of Cazorla, and Don Sancho de Castilla were on guard, the King commanded them to remain at their posts until the Counts of Cabra and Ureña and the Marquis of Astorga entered with their troops, for a certain maneuver. The Moors—who, as I said, stayed up nights trying to disrupt the Christians' construction—led around three thousand infantry and four hundred cavalry up the mountains against Don Rodrigo de Mendoza. The Governor and Don Sancho began to fight against them, when in the thick of the battle the Moors were relieved by many others who came out of the city to help them. King Ferdinand, who was present and witnessed all this, ordered the Count of Tendilla to attack them from the other side, and there ensued a very bloody battle for all. The King, seeing the Count wounded and in danger, ordered the Commander of Santiago to attack on one side and the Marquis of Cádiz, the Duke of Nájera, the governors of Calatrava, and Francisco de Bobadilla to charge with their troops from the side where the artillery lay.

The Moors led a third squad against them and fought most bravely, as did the Christians. When the King found himself in the middle of this struggle, those from his camp noticed and quickly armed themselves to come to his aid. So many rushed to help him

---

Isabella, Luis Fernández Portocarrero, Don Rodrigo de Mendoza, Don Hurtado de Mendoza, and Don Sancho de Castilla, correspond to historical figures active in the war.

that the Moors could not resist them and began to flee with the Christians after them. In their pursuit, the Christians killed a great many and chased the rest to the outskirts of the city. Many soldiers entered Baza, sacking it for great booty, and capturing a few head,[4] among whom was Daraja, a Moorish damsel, the only daughter of the governor of that fortress.

Hers was the most perfect and rare beauty ever seen in a woman. She must have been barely seventeen years of age. If her beauty was of a high degree, her discretion, demeanor, and grace raised her even further. She spoke Spanish so well that it would have been difficult to tell that she was not an Old Christian,[5] for as a fluent speaker she could pass for one.[6] The King was very taken with her, recognizing her great worth. He immediately sent her to his wife, the Queen, who held her in no less esteem and received her happily, as much for her merits—for being the noble descendant of kings and daughter of a most honorable knight—as for the possibility that she might secure the rendition of the city without further injuries or battles. The Queen endeavored to treat her well, favoring her even over those nearest to her person and granting her all their privileges. She embraced her not as a captive but as family, in the hope that such a woman, whose body was so lovely, would not have an ugly soul.

For these reasons the Queen kept her always by her side, and for the pleasure she took in conversing with her, for Daraja described the land to her in great detail, as though she were a much older and wiser man who had seen it all. And although the King and Queen were soon reunited in Baza, once the city had surrendered on certain conditions,

[4] Captives from the defeated city are here counted as though they were cattle, emphasizing their monetary value in the ransom money that would be paid to free them.

[5] As we note in the introduction, in early modern Spain some argued for the superiority of "Old" Christians, whose families had always been Christian, over "New" Christians, who were either recent converts themselves or had been born into a family with Jewish or Moorish origins.

[6] The original uses the term *ladina* for "fluent speaker." In Spain, this term referred to a non-native speaker of Spanish who had mastered it to the point of being almost indistinguishable from a native speaker (Covarrubias 1611, 511) and was used mostly for Spanish-speaking Moors. In the New World, however, it began to be used for acculturated Amerindians and blacks, and thus signaled transformations beyond language proficiency.

the Queen never wished to part with Daraja, so great was the love she bore her. She promised great favors to her father, the Governor, in exchange for her. Daraja's father keenly felt her absence but was heartened by the love the King and Queen had for her, which would result in honor and wealth for her family, and so he did not argue.

The Queen kept Daraja with her always and took her to the city of Seville. She longed for her to become a Christian and prepared her little by little, peacefully and without violence. One day she said, "Daraja, you already know how much I care for you and your pleasure. In return, I ask that you do something for me: exchange your clothes for some of mine that I will give you so that you may enjoy how our dress enhances your beauty."

Daraja answered, "I will gladly do as Your Highness commands. For once I have done as you say, if there is anything worthy in me, from this day forward I will value it more, and indeed it will merit it, for your dress will make it so and supply my faults."

"You come by it naturally," the Queen replied, "I appreciate this service and your good will in offering it."

Daraja dressed in the Castilian fashion and remained in the palace for a few days until the monarchs left to lay siege to the city of Granada. Given the hardships of war and her wish for Daraja to acquire a taste for our faith, the Queen thought it best to leave her in the house of Don Luis de Padilla, a noble knight and a very close confidant of hers, where Daraja might pass the time with his unmarried daughter, Doña Elvira de Guzmán, to whom they entrusted her care. And although Daraja was well cared for there, she felt keenly her absence from her homeland, as well as other, even greater sorrows that she did not disclose. Instead, with a serene look and a happy face, she indicated that Her Highness's pleasure was her own and that she valued her favor.

The damsel's parents had promised her in marriage to a Moorish knight from Granada whose name was Ozmín. His qualities matched Daraja's: he was a rich young man, gallant, intelligent, and, above all, brave and daring, and to each of these qualities one could add a well-deserved *very*. He was as adept at the Spanish tongue as if he had been born and raised in the heart of Castile. That is worth praising in virtuous youth, the glory of their parents, who set their offspring to various languages and noble exercises. He loved his betrothed dearly. In fact, he idolized her so that, if allowed, he would have placed her statue on altars. His memory dwelled on her, his senses lingered on her, and her will was his own. And his betrothed, acknowledging this devotion, responded in kind.

In their love they were equals, as in most other things, and especially in the virtuous dealings they maintained with each other. The sweet words they wrote each other, the loving messages they sent, cannot be praised enough. Although they had seen and visited each other, they had never actually spoken of their love. Yet their eyes often spoke for them, never wasting an opportunity to converse. For many years—not that many, really, given how young they were—since childhood, then, they had loved each other and yearned for each other's visits. True friendship bound their parents, and love their children, so tightly that they all wished to make the bonds familial, as they did through this marriage. Yet it came at a wretched time, and the planets were aligned against it, for no sooner had it been arranged than Baza was besieged.

The disruption and upheaval of the siege led them to postpone the wedding, for they hoped to unite the spouses in a time of greater ease and happiness, and to celebrate the occasion with the games and festivities appropriate for such a joyous event among such distinguished people.

I spoke already of Daraja's father. Her mother was the niece of Boabdelín, the king of that city, on his sister's side, and he had helped arrange the marriage. Ozmín was first cousin to Mohammed, the king of Granada known as the Small King.[7]

Yet things did not turn out as Ozmín wished: fortune proved averse at every turn; Daraja fell under the monarchs' power, and they kept her in Seville. As soon as her betrothed received the news, his laments, his cries, his sighs and manifest sadness moved everyone, and no one

---

[7] Both of these kings were of the Nasrid royal family. Boabdelín, also known as Mohammed al-Zagal, ruled Baza, Guadix, and Almería at the time of the siege of Baza in 1489, while his nephew Boabdil, the Small King, still held power over Granada.

could escape them. Yet since the loss was his alone and the wound so close to his heart, his growing sorrow affected him bodily, and he suffered an illness as difficult to cure as it was to diagnose, with no remedy in sight. He soon seemed on the verge of death, for his symptoms grew as did their cause, and medicine had no effect on him. Worst of all, no one could understand his malady, which was essential in order to cure it. His grief-stricken parents had lost all hope for his recovery; the doctors gave them none, and the symptoms confirmed their opinion.

While everyone suffered, and the sick young man lay almost on his deathbed, he had what seemed a promising idea, though it was risky. Nothing could be more dangerous than the risk he ran at that moment, however, and so, eager to carry it out and longing to see his beloved, he gathered his strength and courage, bravely resisting anything that might harm him. He dismissed sadness and melancholy and focused only on recovering his health. And so his health improved, against all hopes of those who had seen him reach such a sad state. It is truly as they say: desire will always find a way, conquering fear and overcoming all obstacles. Happiness is the best medicine for one who is sick, and so it is wise to find him some; when you see someone happy, consider him cured.

Ozmín soon began to convalesce. He could barely stand when he took as his guide a Moor, an interpreter who had served the kings of Granada for many years as a spy, and gathered jewels and money for the trip. On a good black horse, with a harquebus in the back of his saddle and armed with sword and dagger, he set out from the city at night dressed in Andalusian garb, taking shortcuts along the way, as do those who know the land well.

They passed within sight of the Christian camp and, having left it far behind, headed toward Loja by way of paths and trails. Nearing the city, their miserable fortune led them to a captain rounding up men who had deserted from his troop, fleeing the army. As soon as he saw them, he captured them. The Moor pretended he had a passport, searching for it first in his bosom, then in his purse and all about him. When he failed to find it, and given that they appeared to be lost, the captain became suspicious and arrested them to take them back to the camp.

Ozmín was not in the least perturbed. He freely dropped the name of the knight who held his wife captive, pretending to be his son. He claimed his name was Don Rodrigo de Padilla and that he had come to bring a message to the King and Queen on behalf of his father, as well as news of Daraja. And because he had fallen ill, he was on his way home. He also told the captain he had lost both his passport and his way, and had taken that path in order to return to the road.

It was all to no avail, as the captain still insisted on returning them to the camp, claiming that it made not a cent of difference to him whether they were on their way there or back. He was hoping that a nobleman, such as Ozmín pretended to be, might blind him with some doubloons,[8] for no general's signature can trump the royal seal, especially when it is stamped on one of the nobler metals. Rules apply only to ragged soldiers and turncoats: their superiors show their power by carrying their orders out on them, and not on those from whom they might extract some profit, which is what they truly seek.

Ozmín, who had a sense of where so many threats were headed, said once again, "Do not misunderstand me, Sir: I would not mind returning with you, once or even ten times over, nor would I mind retracing my steps, were it not for my ill health. But since you know my condition, I beg of you not to suffer because my life was placed at risk." And taking from his finger a rich ring, he placed it in the captain's hand.

It was as if he had doused the flames with vinegar, for the captain immediately said: "Go with godspeed, Sir, for clearly such a noble man as you would not take off with the King's pay or forsake the field except for the reasons you give. I shall travel with you to Loja, where I will give orders to ensure that you may carry on safely." And so the captain did, and they became fast friends. Having rested, they said their good-byes, each going his separate way.

After these and other such misfortunes, they arrived in Seville, where, with the information he had, Ozmín soon found out the street and the house where Daraja dwelt. He passed by at different times of day for several days, yet never succeeded in seeing her, as she did not even leave the house to attend church but spent all her time on her handiwork and amusing herself with her friend Doña Elvira.

---

[8] Valuable gold coins stamped with a coat of arms on each side. See the "Note on Coinage" in the introduction.

Ozmín recognized the difficulty of his task and the suspicions he was raising, as strangers usually do anywhere, with all eyes on them, longing to know who they are, where they came from, what they seek, and how they make their living, especially if they frequent the same street and carefully watch windows and doors. This leads to suspicion, rumor grows, and hate builds freely, even if it has nothing to do with them.

Some of this had begun, and so, to avoid scandal, Ozmín was forced to stop for a few days. His servant, who did not merit attention, continued the task. But as he could not see a clear path forward, Ozmín's only consolation came late at night, when he walked down her street embracing the walls, kissing the doors and thresholds of the house.

He lived for some time in this despair until, by chance, the moment he longed for finally arrived. For his servant, taking care to pass by the house several times a day, saw that Don Luis was having a wall repaired, rebuilding it from its foundations. Seizing fortune by the forelock, the servant urged his master to purchase a humble garment and to find some way to get hired as a masonry worker. Ozmín approved of the plan and carried it out. Leaving his servant in charge of his horse and belongings at the inn so that they would be available when he needed them, he headed to the construction site. He asked if there was any work for a foreigner, and they said there was. He certainly did not worry about the wages agreed upon.

He began his task, striving to outwork the others, and although his misfortunes had kept him from a full recovery, he drew—as they say—strength out of weakness, for the heart rules the flesh. He was the first to arrive at work and the last to leave. While the others took their rest, he sought out more tasks. When his fellow workers faulted him for this—for even in misfortune does envy turn up—he claimed that he knew not how to be idle. Don Luis, who noted his diligence, decided to make use of him in the affairs of the house, especially in the garden. He asked Ozmín if he had any skills of that sort; Ozmín responded that he had but few, though his desire to please would soon teach him more. Don Luis was taken with his eloquence and appearance, finding him in all things as capable as he was willing to please.

The mason finished his repairs, and Ozmín stayed on as a gardener.[9] Yet he had never, to that day, managed to see Daraja. On that morning, however, it was his good fortune to have the sun rise bright in a serene and favorable sky, scattering the clouds of his misfortune and shining a new light on the happy haven from all his shipwrecks. On the first afternoon that Ozmín practiced his new office, he saw his betrothed strolling by herself along a wide path bordered with myrtle, musk rose, jasmine, and other flowers, some of which she gathered to adorn her hair.

He would not have known her in her new attire, if the true original had not matched the vivid image inscribed in his soul. And he realized such great beauty could only be hers. He was too unsettled to speak to her as she passed, and so bowed his head, bashful and tongue-tied, working the earth with the hoe in his hand. Daraja looked again at the new gardener. The side of his face, which was what she could see readily, recalled that on which her imagination always dwelt, for he resembled her betrothed so closely. This brought her such sudden grief that she fell to the ground. Holding onto a garden trellis, she gave a distressed sigh, accompanied by infinite tears. Putting her hand to her rosy cheek, she recalled many things, any of which, had she dwelt on it, could have served as her executioner.

She dismissed these memories as best she could with a new desire to comfort her soul with the sight of the gardener, deceiving it with what little resemblance to Ozmín he bore. She stood up, her whole body trembling and her heart in anguish, to contemplate once again the image she adored, for the more closely she looked at him, the more vividly the image turned into him. She thought it was a dream, yet she could see that she was awake, and so feared he was a ghost. Realizing that he was a man, she hoped only that he would turn out to be the one she loved. She remained perplexed and doubtful, unable to grasp what he was, for his illness had left him thin and devoid of his usual color, while everything else—his features, his stance, his

___

[9] By the 1590s, both masons and gardeners—the two disguises that Ozmín adopts here—would have been stereotypically associated with Moriscos. There may be an oblique reminder here of the connection between the idealized Moors of the text and their persecuted brethren in the late sixteenth century.

manner—confirmed that it was he. Yet his office, his attire, and the very place where he stood banished her hopes and disabused her of them. She was sorry to have seen the truth of the matter, and yet she persevered in her desire, unable to prevent a special affection for him, given whom he resembled. And in her doubt and anxiousness to know who he was, she asked him, "Brother, where are you from?"

Ozmín raised his head to see his exquisite and sweet beloved. His tongue knotted in his throat and left him unable to utter a word or to give an answer so that his eyes spoke for him, watering the ground with the many tears that sprung from them as if from two reservoirs whose gates had been lifted. And so the two lovers recognized each other.

Daraja responded in the same manner, and strings of pearls ran down her cheeks. They longed to embrace, or at least to exchange some sweet and loving words, when Don Rodrigo, the eldest son of Don Luis, entered the scene. As he was in love with Daraja, he followed her every footstep, seeking any opportunity to contemplate her beauty. To avoid suspicion, Ozmín returned to his work while Daraja continued on her way.

From her sad countenance and burning eyes, Don Rodrigo could tell that something had occurred. He suspected something had upset her and asked Ozmín about it. Even though he himself had not recovered from his emotion, Ozmín forced himself to do so out of necessity and responded: "Sir, the way you see her now is the way she looked when she arrived. She did not exchange a word with me, and so did not tell me, nor do I know, what has upset her so. And especially as this is my first day in this place, it would not have been fitting for me to ask, nor for her in her discretion to tell me."

With this, Don Rodrigo moved on, intent on asking Daraja herself; but while he had paused to exchange these words with Ozmín, she had quickly mounted a spiral staircase to her chambers and closed the door behind her.

The lovers spent several mornings and afternoons in this manner, enjoying at times some of the flowers and honest fruits of the tree of love, with which they relieved their sadness, contemplating their true pleasure, and longing for that happy time when they could freely enjoy each other without shadows or impediments. Yet they did not long enjoy even these pleasures, or at least not very safely, for the length of their conversations, the sight of them speaking together in Arabic, and the fact that Daraja excused herself from the company of her friend Doña Elvira to do so soon vexed everyone in the house, and especially Don Rodrigo, who was filled with angry concern. He was consumed by jealousy, not because he believed the gardener could be discussing anything illicit or amorous with her but simply because he was worthy of such frequent sweet conversation with Daraja, which she would have with none other so freely.

Rumor, the natural daughter of hate and envy, always seeks to taint the lives of others, sullying their virtues. And so for those of base and lowly condition, among whom she keeps her court, it is the most delectable sauce, without which no meat seems tasty or well seasoned. It is the swiftest bird, for it pounces most speedily and causes the most harm. There was no lack of people to pass the word from hand to hand, some adding to and others elaborating on their great familiarity until the ball dropped and the rumor reached the ears of Don Luis, carried by those who thought it would bring them advantage as their lord's honored favorites. This is what the world practices: to curry favor with their betters at the expense of others through connivance and lies, if the truth gives them no ground for achieving what they desire. A fitting office for those with no virtue of their own and whose works and persons are of no worth!

Don Luis listened to these well-composed and embellished words. He was a wise and prudent gentleman, and so did not let them linger where they had been set before him but sent them on to his imagination, leaving room for what the accused might say. He kept an open mind and would not allow it to be closed, even though he was somewhat alarmed. He had many thoughts, all of them far from the truth, and what most troubled him was the suspicion that his gardener might be a Moor cunningly trying to steal Daraja away. Convinced that this was the case, he was immediately blinded to any other possibility. And as is often the case with rash decisions, no sooner have they been acted upon than regret sets in. Yet with this suspicion Don Luis resolved to arrest Ozmín.

Ozmín did not show sorrow or alarm, nor did he resist, but allowed himself to be locked in a room. Leaving him thus secured, Don Luis went to Daraja, who from the uproar of the assistants and servants already knew everything that had occurred and had even predicted it for some days. She came to Don Luis very aggrieved, complaining that the goodness and chastity of her life had been cast into doubt, with such a smear as would allow anyone to think whatever he wished, for the door had been left wide open to all bad suspicions.

These and other well-considered reasons, affectingly delivered, easily led Don Luis to feel remorse for what he had done. He now wished, after Daraja had chastised him, that he had never brought up such matters, and he berated himself and those who had put him up to it. In order not to seem fickle, however, and to avoid admitting that he had acted on such a grave issue without due consideration, he disguised his regret as he responded:

"Dear Daraja, I fully grant that you are right and recognize how wrongfully this matter was pursued, without having first examined the motives of the witnesses who testified against you. I know your worth, that of your parents, and that of the ancestors from whom you descend. I know your own merits have elicited from the King and Queen, my lords, all the love that a true and only child can inspire in her devoted parents, and that they have showed you their bountiful and well-known favor. Yet you must acknowledge that they placed you in my house so you could be served with the utmost care and diligence according to your will, and that I will be held accountable for you according to the trust that was placed in me. Because of this and of my desire to serve you, you must act in kind, according to who you are, with the good treatment that my loyalty deserves. I cannot, nor do I want to, believe that you could be capable of anything that is not honorable. But the great familiarity you have with Ambrosio (for this was the name Ozmín took when he began work as a laborer) has raised some concern, as has your speaking to each other in Arabic, which makes everyone want to know what it means and how it started, given that neither you nor I had ever seen or known him before. If these questions were answered, you would dispel many of their doubts and quiet in me an impertinent and profound unease. I beg of you, for who you are, to relieve us of this doubt and to believe that, insofar as possible, I will always be at your service in all that you desire."

Daraja listened intently to what Don Luis was saying so that she could respond, even though her sharp mind had already prepared explanations in her defense in case something were to be discovered. But in this short while, she was forced to leave aside her previous excuses and to rely on others more pertinent to what was asked of her so that he might be reassured and relax his vigilance. With great foresight, and in order to continue taking pleasure in her betrothed as she was wont to do, she said:

"My lord and father, for so I may call you—lord, for I am in your power, and father, for your treatment of me—I would ignore my obligation for the continual favors I receive from their Majesties by your own hand, and through your intercessions on my behalf, which increase them, if I did not entrust my greatest secrets to the repository of your discretion, finding refuge in your shadow and taking your good sense for my rule, and if I did not satisfy you with the truth itself. For even though recalling the things I must relate will cause me great sorrow and no small amount of suffering, I want to repay you in this way and lay my sorrow at your feet, and reassure you that I obey your commands.

"By now, my lord, you have come to know who I am, and that my misfortune or my good luck—I cannot condemn one thing or praise another until I see the fruit of so many trials—brought me to your house after my marriage had been arranged to one of the most esteemed knights of Granada, a close relative and descendant of its kings. This husband of mine, if I may call him that, was raised from the time he was six or seven years old with another boy, a Christian captive of the same age, whom his parents purchased for his service and entertainment. They were together constantly, played together, ate and slept together, all for the love they had for each other. See, my lord, whether these were not the pledges of true friendship! My husband loved him as if he had been his equal or his relative. He entrusted his person to him, for he was so brave; he was the storehouse of his pleasures, his companion in entertainments, treasury of his secrets—in essence, another of him. The two were so similar in all respects that only their religion set them apart, which, for they were both very wise, they never discussed, to avoid straining their brotherly bond.

"The captive—truly, I should call him brother—deserved this treatment for his loyalty, his upstanding manners, and his noble behavior. Had we not known that he had been born to humble laborers, who were captured with him on a lowly farm, we would have thought he was descended from some noble bloodline and generous household. This man, once our marriage had been arranged, carried all messages between us and was so loyal in that task that he did nothing else. He would bring me letters and gifts, and return with the due response. He was in Baza when it was captured, and so he was freed along with most of the captives who were found there. Yet I cannot say whether the joy of gaining his liberty was as great as his pain at having lost us. You may easily ask him for yourself, along with anything else you might want to know, because he is Ambrosio, the one you have in your service, where, God being served, he came to relieve my sorrow. I lost him without quite knowing how, and by chance, I have found him again. With him I review the courses of my disgrace, in which I have now attained my degree. With him I tend the hopes of my adverse fortune and distract myself from a sorrowful life, to disguise the weariness of time's slow passing. If this consolation, which is for my good, offends you, then do as you will, for my will follows yours."

Don Luis was astonished and moved, as much by the strangeness as by the sadness of the case, and by the way it was recounted—without any pause, hesitation, or mistake from which one might assume that Daraja was making it up as she went along. She gave even more credit to her story by shedding some effective tears, which would have softened the hardest stone or cut the finest diamond. And so Ambrosio was released from prison without a single question, so as not to cast doubt on the information Daraja had given. Simply placing his arms around Ambrosio's neck, Don Luis happily announced:

"I now know, Ambrosio, that you must come from noble blood, and if you did not, your own virtues and nobility would stand in for it. What I have learned about you now obliges me to treat you as you deserve."

Ozmín responded: "In this, Sir, you shall act as befits you, and any favor I might receive I will treasure as coming from your generosity and your house."

With this, Ozmín was allowed to return to the garden with the same familiarity as he had first enjoyed and with even more license. Now he and Daraja could speak to each other as often as they wished without scandalizing anyone any longer.

Meanwhile, the King and Queen always took care to inquire about Daraja's health and well-being, of which they were carefully apprised. They enjoyed hearing about her and always remembered her in their letters. This royal favor was so powerful that, in their longing for influence as much as for the damsel's own merits, Don Rodrigo and the other principal lords of that city wished to make her Christian and courted her for their wife. But because Don Rodrigo had her—as they say—in-house, he had the best chance among them all, according to common opinion. The case was simple and their suspicion well founded: she had already experienced his condition,[10] manners, and demeanor, and the display of such qualities is hardly insignificant, nor is it a small step to display one's virtues and nobility in public, so as to be known and favored. But as the lovers had already exchanged souls and no longer possessed their own, they were as loyal in their love as they were averse to hurting one another. Daraja was never bold, nor did she offer any excuse that would invite any amorous advances, even though they all adored her. And so each one tried to find his own way, slowly casting his nets, yet none had any reason to hope.

Don Rodrigo was aware of what little use his attentions had proved, how fruitless his efforts, and how slim his hopes—for after the many days he had spent in continuous conversation with Daraja he was no further than he had been on the first. And so it occurred to him to use Ozmín, thinking that through his intercession he might achieve some favors. Seeking them through the most likely means, he said to Ozmín one morning in the garden,

"You are well aware, my brother Ambrosio, of your obligations to your religion, your king, and your country, as well as for the bread my parents' provide you, and for all our good wishes for you. I believe that, as a Christian of the quality that your actions demonstrate, you will act

---

[10] "Condition" here refers to someone's perceived position in society, that is, whether someone is "rich, or poor, noble, or plebeian" (Covarrubias 1611, 231).

according to who you are. I come to you with a particular need—the increase of my honor and my very life depend on it, both of which are in your hands. I beg you to speak with Daraja and convince her to leave the false sect and turn Christian, adding your own persuasions to other reasons. You know full well the good that would come of this: salvation for Daraja, good service unto God, fulfillment for the King and Queen, honor to your country, and a complete cure for me. Requesting her as my wife, I will marry her, and this will benefit you as well, bringing you not just honor but as handsome a profit as your intelligence might conceive, because God will honor you for the soul you win over, and I, for my part, will reward you fully for saving my life and interceding on my behalf with favors and friendship. Do not refuse me, since you can do so much with her. I should not press you any further when so many obligations compel you to do this."

When Don Rodrigo had finished his exhortation, Ozmín responded as follows:

"The same reason with which you seek to bind me, Don Rodrigo, will make you believe how much I long for Daraja to follow my faith, as I have countless, multiple times persuaded her. My own wish in this matter is none other than your own, and so I will do as you ask for my own sake, in a matter that so concerns me. Yet she so loves her husband, and my lord, that to try to turn her Christian is to redouble her passion to no end, for she still harbors hope for a change of fortune that might let her have her way. This is what she has told me and what she has always said, and I have seen her hold to it. Yet to follow your command, fruitless though it may be, I shall talk to her again and discuss it with her, and give you her answer."

The Moor had not lied at all in what he said, had his true meaning been understood. Not remotely suspecting anything so far from his own purpose, however, Don Rodrigo believed what Ozmín had actually said instead of what he had meant to convey. And so, deceived in this way, Don Rodrigo felt newly confident, for he who truly loves finds hope in hopelessness.

Ozmín was so distressed to discover these attempts against him that he almost lost his wits from jealousy. The news so oppressed him that from then on he was never cheerful, as the impossible became possible in his mind. He wrestled with his thoughts, imagining that this new rival, so powerful in his land and in his household, and so determined, would have tricks and strategies to hinder Ozmín's own plan. Ozmín feared they might change his Daraja, for battering rams breach strong walls and secret mines level them and ruin them. With these misgivings, his thoughts ran to tragic ends and terrible events, all of which took shape in his mind. He did not so much believe them as he feared them greatly, as would any perfect lover.

When Daraja saw her beloved husband so dejected for so long, she longed to know the cause; but he neither told her nor spoke a word of what had occurred with Don Rodrigo. She did not know what to do nor how to cheer him, but spoke to him with sweet words and good cheer, uttered with a soft tone and a firm heart, and underscored by her beautiful eyes, which softened her features with the tears that flowed from them:

"Lord of my liberty, god whom I adore, and husband whom I obey, what has such power to torment you when I am alive and in your presence? Is my life perhaps the price of your happiness? Or what would you do with it so that my soul might escape the hell of your sadness in which it now suffers? Let the sun of your happy countenance scatter the clouds in my heart! If my entreaties mean anything, if my love for you deserves any consideration, if the sorrows I endure move you at all, if you do not wish my life to be buried in your secret, I beg you to tell me what makes you so sad."

Here she stopped, drowning in tears, as her words had a similar effect on Ozmín, who could only respond with burning, loving tears of his own. They tried with their own tears to wash away those of the other, until their tears became as one, for their tongues could not speak.

Crushed by his own sighs, but fearing they would be heard, Ozmín so repressed them, trying to return them to his soul, that he fainted away as if dead. Daraja did not know what to do, how to rouse him or console him, nor could she conceive the cause of such a change in one who had always been so cheerful. She busied herself with cleaning his face, drying his eyes and placing her beautiful hands on them, having wet a precious handkerchief that she held, embroidered with gold and silver and many other colors, and woven with small and large pearls of great worth. She was so altered by this new sorrow, and so wholly caught up in remedying it, that Don Rodrigo almost found them there all but embracing. Daraja had his head on her knee, and Ozmín was resting on her skirts when he came to himself. Just as Ozmín recovered, and while he was preparing to say good-bye, Don Rodrigo entered the garden.

Daraja, in her confusion, withdrew as best she could, leaving behind on the ground her rare handkerchief, which was quickly retrieved by her lord. And when she saw that Don Rodrigo was approaching, she took her leave and left the two men alone. Don Rodrigo asked Ozmín what he had worked out. Ozmín responded as he had before:

"I find her so firm in her love for her husband that not only will she not become a Christian, as you hope, but for his sake she would cease to be one if she were, becoming a Moor instead, so extreme is her madness, her love for her religion and for her husband. I presented your offer, but she so hates you for attempting it and me for proposing it that she has determined not to see me if I speak of it again. And when she saw you approach, she fled. So do not insist nor waste your time on this matter, for it will be all in vain."

Don Rodrigo was disheartened by so resolute an answer, so harshly delivered. He suspected Ozmín was actually working against him rather than in his favor. It seemed to him that even if Daraja had given such a distasteful response, Ozmín should not have relayed it in that manner, as though it were his affair. So we see that love and discretion rarely go together: the more one loves, the more one comes undone. Don Rodrigo recalled the very close friendship that Ozmín was said to have with his former master: that flame, he surmised, still burned, and the ashes of that fire had probably not grown cold. With this thought, and bolstered by his passion, Don Rodrigo resolved to dismiss Ozmín from the house, telling his father how dangerous it was to allow Daraja near someone who would recall her past love and discuss it with her, especially as it was their Majesties' intent to turn her Christian, which would be hard to do as long as Ambrosio was present. "Let us," he said, "try separating them, Sir, and see what comes of it."

His son's counsel did not displease Don Luis. Right away, inventing complaints where none were warranted—for the powerful do not need to justify themselves, and the captain with his soldiers does as he pleases, so that two and two make three—he dismissed Ozmín from his house, commanding him not to set foot in the door again. This took Ozmín by surprise, and he was not even able to bid Daraja good-bye. Obeying his master, and feigning less sorrow than what he felt, he dragged away his body, which was all he could take with him, for his soul remained with her in whose power it had long rested.

When Daraja learned of this sudden change, she assumed that Ozmín's former sorrow must have come from his misgivings about it and that he had already known it was to occur. So one blow joined with the next, sorrow with sorrow and grief with grief. Although the poor lady dissembled as best she could, what hurt her most was to lose all chance of seeing her husband. Let the afflicted cry, moan, sigh, shout, and carry on, for if this does not dispel their suffering, at least it may alleviate it and somewhat lessen it. Daraja so lacked for all happiness that she lost all pleasure and taste for things, and her sorrow could be clearly read in her face and manner.

Our Moorish lover did not wish to change his condition. Dressed as before, in the habit of a day laborer, he followed his weary fortune. In this dress, he had known good luck, and he hoped for even better. He worked for wages wherever he could, trying his luck as he went from place to place. In this way, he hoped to learn something useful, and only for this reason did he do it, as he could have lived well for a long time on the money and jewels he had taken from his house. Yet for this reason, and given that he had already shown himself in dress that gave him free rein, allowing him to go undetected and protecting his designs, he carried on with it for the time being.

The young knights who served Daraja, knowing how she favored Ozmín and that he was no longer a servant in Don Luis's house, all coveted him for their own ends, which they soon made public. Don Alonso de Zúñiga, a rich heir in that city and an honorable, gallant, and wealthy knight, took the lead, confident that necessity, his riches, and his recourse to Ambrosio would grant him victory. He sent for him, agreed on terms, did him many good turns, and showered him with praise. And so they began a kind of friendship—if such a thing can exist between master and servant, for though it is possible insofar as they are men, in this situation it is generally known as favor.

After several attempts, Don Alonso revealed his desire to Ozmín, promising him great rewards. All this opened Ozmín's wounds and inflamed his sores, making them worse. If before he had been jealous of one, now there were two; soon he learned of many others whom his master revealed to him, what paths they took, and whose assistance they sought. For his part, Don Alonso claimed, he did not want or seek any help beyond Ozmín's good intelligence, for he was certain that his intercession alone would be enough to achieve his end.

I could not express, nor could anyone truly imagine, what Ozmín felt when asked once again to play the pander for his wife and how important it was for him to carry on with discreet dissembling. He responded kindly to Don Alonso, lest what had happened with Don Rodrigo should occur again. Had he challenged them all while he still had such a long way to go, he would have lost everything and learned nothing. Patience and sufferance are required to reach one's ends peacefully. So he continued to distract Don Alonso, burning alive all the while. He battled his own thoughts, which assaulted him from all sides and covered him with blows, so that he did not know where to turn or whom to follow, nor could he find any comfort to ease his torments.

There was a single hare, and the hounds were many and swift, aided by falcons of the house, female friends, acquaintances, banquets, and visits, such as often set fire to honor. For to many honorable houses there come those who appear to be ladies and yet who cease to be so while on their supposed visit, whether because of their own need or by trickery, for all of this goes on. Noble and grave people were not neglected when the devil procured bawds and bodies.

Ozmín feared all this, but above all he feared Don Rodrigo, whom he and the other rivals hated for his false arrogance. Don Rodrigo tried to dissuade them with his manner, hoping to convince them that it was born of Daraja's favor and that they should therefore desist. Meanwhile, they spoke to him kindly but did not love him. Their mouths dripped with honey while their hearts harbored poison, and they held him to their hearts while longing to tear his to pieces. They smiled at him as dogs grin at a wasp, for so it is in this day and age, especially among the great.

Let us now return to the torments that Daraja suffered and her efforts to learn of her husband's fate—where he had gone, what had become of him, if he was in good health, how he spent his time, if he loved elsewhere. This last concern troubled her the most, for even though mothers, too, fear for their absent sons, there is a difference: a mother fears for the life of her son, while a wife fears for the love of her husband, worried that another woman might be distracting him with caresses and flattery. How sad were those days for Daraja, how long those nights, how she wove and unwove her thoughts, as Penelope did her cloth, with her chaste desire for her beloved Ulysses![11]

Here I will say most by remaining silent. For to depict such sadness, not even the trick used by a famous painter would do. At the death of a maiden, he painted her in her place, and surrounded her with parents, siblings, relatives, friends, acquaintances, and the servants of the house, each in their place and showing the sadness befitting their condition. Yet when he came to her parents, he left their faces unfinished, allowing the viewers to paint for themselves the pain they might feel. For there are no words nor brushes to express the love or the sorrow that parents feel, but only certain deeds among the gentiles, of which we have read.[12] So will I do. My coarse tongue would be but a broad brush that could only paint blots. Best then to leave it to the discretion of the listeners, and to those who know the story, to consider how such passions are felt. They should imagine it for themselves, judging the heart of another by their own.

Daraja was so sad that her demeanor betrayed her inner feelings. Seeing her in such an extreme state of melancholy, Don Luis and his son Don Rodrigo ordered some bullfights and riding games[13] to cheer

---

[11] The narrator here mentions explicitly the parallels with Homer's *Odyssey*, strongly suggested in the descriptions of the suitors vying for Daraja's attention while Ozmín moves about them in disguise.

[12] The author may refer here to the practice of hiring *plañideras* to weep at funerals as a means of producing catharsis in the crowd. This practice is described in the Book of Lamentations (Jeremiah 9:17).

[13] The *juegos de cañas* (games of canes) that Alemán refers to here were immensely popular among the nobility in early modern Spain, particularly in Andalusia. Of Andalusi origin, the games involved richly attired quadrilles that performed elaborate maneuvers on horseback and threw light reeds at each other.

her up. Because the city was so well suited to these pastimes, they soon came about. The quadrilles gathered, each one dressed in silks of different colors, with which each of the riders revealed his feelings: some showed their despair, others, their hope; some, their enthrallment, others, their doubt; some, their joy, others, their sadness; some, their jealousy, others, their love. But Daraja responded to all alike.

When Ozmín learned of the planned festivities and that his master would participate in the quadrilles, he decided to waste no time in seeing his wife and to show his worth by distinguishing himself on that occasion. When the day came, and just as the bulls began to run, he entered on his mount, both well fitted. He had covered his face with blue taffeta and his horse's eyes with a black band. He pretended to be a foreigner. His servant went before him, bearing his thick lance. He circled the entire plaza, beholding the many marvelous things that were there. Among them all, Daraja's beauty shone as the day does against the night. Her presence threw everything else into shadow. He placed himself near her window and from there saw the whole plaza in a commotion as the crowd ran from the threat of a famously fierce bull that they had just let loose. He was from Tarifa, large, malicious, and fierce as a lion.

As soon as he stepped out, the bull reached the middle of the plaza in two or three bounds, bestriding it and frightening all who were there. He turned his head in all directions, and they threw some canes at him. Shaking them off, he artfully prevented them from throwing any more from below, striking out at a few and missing none. They no longer dared to take him on, nor was there a soul who would challenge him on foot, even from very far away. Thus they left him alone, with no one but the enamored Ozmín and his servant standing by.

The bull then charged like the wind, and Ozmín had to take up his lance with no delay, for the bull admitted none in his charge. He held high his arm, around which he had knotted Daraja's handkerchief, and with graceful dexterity and a gallant air he stabbed the bull through the back of the neck, piercing his whole body and nailing his left hoof to the ground. There he left him quite dead, as though made of stone and no longer moving at all. Ozmín himself was left with a piece of the lance in his hand, which he cast to the ground as he left the plaza. Daraja was overjoyed to see him—she had recognized him as soon as he rode in because of his servant, who had also been hers, and then by the handkerchief on his arm.

Everyone was left murmuring admiration and praise, impressed by the fortunate blow and the strength of the masked man. No one could talk of anything else. They had all seen it, and yet they all wanted to tell the story. They all thought it had been but a dream, and yet they could not stop recounting it again and again: one person clapping, others shouting and gesturing. One stands amazed, another crosses himself, yet another raises his hands, their mouths and eyes full of joy. One bends over and leaps up; some raise their eyebrows; others, bursting with pleasure, do an antic dance. . . . All of this was for Daraja a greater glory.

Ozmín withdrew to some orchards outside the city, from which he had come before. Leaving his horse, he changed his dress but kept his sword at his side. Becoming Ambrosio once again, he returned to the plaza. He stood where he could see what he desired and where he could be seen by one who loved him more than her own life. They rejoiced in beholding each other, though Daraja was fearful that some harm could come to him, as he was on foot. She signaled that he should stand on a scaffold. He pretended he did not understand her and remained there for the rest of the bullfights.

As the evening drew near, the quadrilles for the games of canes entered in the following manner: first came the trumpets, shawms, and drums in their colorful liveries, and behind them followed eight mules carrying bundles of canes. They belonged to the eight quadrilles that would play, and each was covered with a velvet cloth bearing the arms of its owner embroidered in gold and silk. They were secured with cords of gold and silk with silver ties.

Next came 240 horses belonging to 48 knights—5 for each, not counting the one he started on, which made 6 in total. The horses that were led in first came in two lines from opposite directions. The first two were paired together, and the rest were organized into groups of five, which bore on the arson of their saddles, facing outward, their owners' shields, upon which were painted emblems and mottos, with ribbons and tassels, each according to his fancy. The rest of the horses wore only harnesses with bells and rich, rare trappings: proud bridles of gold and silver with the most precious stonework, beyond all description. What more can I say than that this all took place in Seville, where there is no lack of such things or expertise in them, and that the knights were lovers, rivals, rich, and young—and their lady was present.

They entered through one gate and, after circling the entire plaza, left through another next to the one they had used before, so that those who were going out did not hinder those who were coming in, and in this way they all paraded by. Once the horses were gone, the knights came in again, with the eight quadrilles running two by two. Their liveries were as I have described, and in their hands they held their lances, shaking them so that the stock and the point blurred together and each one appeared to be four. The horses were encouraged with loud shouts. Nudged with sharp spurs, they fairly flew, with each rider so close on his saddle that they seemed to be a single body. This is no exaggeration, for in most of Andalusia—in Seville, Córdoba, Jerez de la Frontera—children are placed—so they say—from the cradle onto the saddle, just as in other places they are given hobbyhorses to ride. It is a wonder to see such hard steel and such dexterity at such tender ages, for they think nothing of hurting their mounts.

They circled the plaza, galloping around all four sides, then exited and made another entrance as they had before. But this time, having changed horses, they wore their shields on their arms and held their canes in their hands. They took their places in groups of six, as is the custom of the land, and began a handsome, well-ordered game. After about a quarter of an hour had passed in this way, another group of knights entered the game to break them up, beginning another organized skirmish with new horses. One side and the other showed such precision that it looked like a concerted dance, which all watched in suspenseful pleasure.

This sport was interrupted by a furious bull that they released as the grand finale. Those who were on horseback took up their pikes and began to surround him. The bull stood still, not knowing which way to charge: he looked around at all of them, tearing at the ground with his hooves. And while each awaited his fate, a rascal ran out from the crowd and began goading him on, gesturing and making faces.

It did not take him long to make the bull, as if enraged, abandon those on horseback and charge toward him. The boy turned in flight and the bull followed, until he was right below Daraja's windows, where Ozmín also stood. Ozmín felt that the boy had sought refuge in a special place and that any harm that came to him there would dishonor both his lady and himself. In light of this, and given his fury at those who had wanted to show off their talents there that day, Ozmín broke through the crowd and charged the bull who, leaving his previous target, ran toward him. Everyone thought that a man who would charge such a beast, and with such conviction, must be mad, and they fully expected to extract him in pieces from between the bull's horns.

Everyone yelled at him in loud voices to be careful. Imagine the state his betrothed was in—I cannot describe it except to say that she was a woman bereft of her soul and insensible from feeling so much. The bull lowered his head to gore Ozmín but actually turned out to be humbling himself in sacrifice, as he would never raise it again. For the Moor moved his body to the side, and simultaneously, with extraordinary dexterity, unsheathed his sword, plunging it through the animal's neck. Shattering the skull, he left the head hanging from the gullet and jowls, and there the bull lay dead. Then, as if he had done nothing at all, he sheathed his sword and left the plaza.

But the curious and common crowd, horsemen as well as footmen, began to close in on him from all sides to discover his identity. So many crowded him in admiration that they almost suffocated him, and he could not take a step. From windows and scaffolds, there arose another chorus of admiration much like the first, with widespread excitement. And because they had happened as the festivities were ending, the crowd spoke of nothing else but the two marvels of that afternoon, debating which had been greater and expressing gratitude for the delightful last course they had been offered, which had left their palates and their mouths full of relish to recount such feats for time immemorial.

As you might imagine, on this day, Daraja's own pleasures were interrupted, her joy marred with grief, her good news proven false, and her relish soured. Barely had she seen what she longed for, when she was struck by the fear of danger. She did not know when she would see him next nor how to calm her heart, satisfying the hunger of her eyes with the sweet taste of her desire, and the very thought tortured her. Pleasure cannot live where sorrow lingers, and so no one could tell from the look on her face or even by speaking to her if the festivities had entertained her. Yet the gallant suitors were even wilder for her than before, aroused by Daraja's great beauty, desirous to know how best to please her and to see her again. In the heat of their pride, they called for a joust, declaring Don Rodrigo the challenger.

The challenge was posted a few nights later, with so much music and so many torches that the streets and plazas seemed ablaze. They placed it where it would be visible to all, and easily legible. There was a tiltyard near the city wall, next to what is known as the Córdoba gate—I saw it in my own time, though in poor condition—where knights would go to practice their jousts. There Don Alonso de Zúñiga, who was new to such things, practiced among the rest. He was eager to distinguish himself since he was so taken by Daraja.

He was afraid to lose the tournament and admitted it freely, not because he lacked the will or the strength but because practice is what makes experts of men and theory alone fools the most confident of them. He did not wish to err and so proceeded modestly and carefully. Ozmín, for his part, wanted to have as few enemies as possible, and since he could not joust nor would he be admitted, he wanted someone to enter the lists who might overthrow Don Rodrigo's pride, since he was more wary of him than of all the rest. With this in mind, rather than to serve his master, Ozmín said to him: "My lord, if you give me license to speak, I will tell you something that may benefit you on this honorable occasion."

Don Alonso, distracted and without the slightest idea that he might be referring to the joust, assumed instead that Ozmín had something to tell him about his love, and so said, "Get on with it, then. I long to hear what you have to say."

"I see, my lord," Ozmín said, "that you must participate in the announced festivities of this tournament. And it is no surprise that, when a glorious name is at stake, the great longing to secure it might daunt a man. I, your servant, will help you, quickly training you in whatever you wish to know of chivalry and the use of arms so that my lessons are fruitful for you. Do not let my youth surprise or scandalize you because I was raised to this and so know a thing or two about it."

Don Alonso was delighted at what he heard, and, thanking him, said, "If you can deliver what you offer, I will be greatly in your debt."

Ozmín replied: "He who promises what he does not plan to keep ventures far from his word, and seeks only to distract and make excuses. But he who, like myself, cannot make any such moves, must deliver even more than he promises, unless he is a fool. Order them, my lord, to prepare weapons for you and for me, and soon you shall see how much longer I have taken to make this promise than I shall take in fulfilling it, though doing so will not free me of the obligation to serve you."

Don Alonso quickly ordered the necessary equipment, and when it was ready, they headed to a secluded place where they dedicated that day and most of those remaining until the tournament to practicing. Soon enough, Don Alonso was so steady in his saddle and good with his lance, which he took out with such a skilled air and carried with such grace, that it seemed as if he had been practicing for many years. In addition to all the practice, the grace of his body and his good strength were most important and helped him accordingly.

Ozmín's talent for riding both kinds of saddles[14] and for carrying out the lessons, as well as his figure, composure, behavior, habits, and manner of speaking, all led Don Alonso to think that his name could not actually be Ambrosio and much less could he be a mere worker. Instead, his whole person was carefully wrought. His actions betrayed the polish of a principal and noble person who, because of some turn of events, was going about in this fashion. Unable to contain himself until he could resolve the matter, Don Alonso took Ozmín aside and said to him privately: "Ambrosio, though you have served me for only a short while, I owe you much. Your virtues and your manners reveal who you are so clearly that you cannot disguise it. Under the veil of that base suit you wear, and under those clothes, that occupation, that name, there lies another person hidden. It is clear to me from the evidence you have given me that you are deceiving me, or rather that you were deceiving me. For the poor laborer that you pretend to be would

---

[14] The *jineta* saddle, with short stirrup leathers, was often associated with the Andalusi style of riding, and more broadly with Spain, whereas the *brida*, with long stirrup leathers, was associated with France.

never know so much, particularly about chivalry, especially being as young as you are. I have seen through you, and I know that under those clods of earth and muddy shells lie the finest gold and oriental pearls. It is patent to you who I am and most unclear to me who you are, even though, as I said, causes are known by their effects, and you cannot conceal yourself from me. I swear to you by the faith that I have in Jesus Christ and the order of chivalry that I profess to be your faithful and secret friend, keeping whatever you entrust to me and helping you with whatever my person or my purse can provide. Tell me of your fortunes, so that I may somehow repay the good deeds you have done for me."

Ozmín replied: "My lord, you have conjured me so powerfully and so tightened the screws that I must wring from my soul what only your noble manner could extract. So, to obey your orders, and trusting in who you are and what you have promised, I must tell you that I am a knight from Zaragoza in Aragon. My name is Jaime Vives, son of a father of the same name. A few years ago, it so happened that I fell into the hands of Moors and was taken captive due to the conniving of false friends. Whether it was because of their envy or my misfortune is a long story. While I was in their power, they sold me to a renegade,[15] and by that name you can imagine the treatment I received. He took me inland to Granada, where a noble Zegrí knight[16] bought me. He had a son my age named Ozmín, who was the very picture of myself; we were alike in age as in stature, features, condition, and kind. And because I so resembled his son, he was intent on buying me and treating me well, leading to a greater amity between us. I taught him what I knew and what I could, according to what I had learned from my people in my own land and from our frequent practice of such exercises. From this I reaped no small benefit, for in discussing those exercises with my master's son, I learned more about what I might otherwise have forgotten, for those who teach learn. So both father and son grew fonder of me and began to entrust me with their persons and their wealth. This

[15] "Renegade" (or *renegado*, used in early modern English, too) referred to Christians who abandoned their Christian faith for Islam. The word derives from the Spanish verb *renegar* (to reject or deny), which refers to the action of declaring oneself apostate.

[16] The Zegrí family was a noble clan in Al-Andalus memorialized (along with the Abencerrajes) in Ginés Pérez de Hita's *Civil Wars of Granada*.

young man was betrothed to Daraja, daughter of the mayor of Baza, my lady whom you so adore. The wedding was about to occur, and it would have taken place as their agreement stipulated had the siege and the wars not impeded it. They were forced to postpone it, and then Baza surrendered and the wedding was left in suspense. Because I was their confidant, I exchanged gifts and presents between them from one city to the other. I was fortunate to be in Baza when the city surrendered, and so I recovered my liberty with all the other captives there. I longed to return to my land but had no money to do so. I heard that a relative of mine lived in this city, and so two things came together: my desire to see a place so illustrious and magnificent and my hope to improve my lot in order to continue on my way. I was here for a long time without finding the person I sought, because the information I had received had been uncertain. What was certain, however, was my own perdition, for I found what I was not seeking, as is often the case. I was wandering through the city, with little money and great cares, when I saw a rare beauty, or at least so she appeared to my eyes, though she may not to those of others, for only what pleases us is beautiful. I surrendered completely, and my soul left me; I no longer knew myself and I was entirely hers. I refer to Doña Elvira, sister to Don Rodrigo and daughter to Don Luis de Padilla, my lord. As they say, necessity is the mother of invention, and so finding myself so lost in love and with no way to demonstrate it with the actual qualities of my person, I decided to write my father to tell him that I owed a thousand double doubloons[17] for my liberty and to ask him to help me with them. This plan worked out well, for he sent them to me along with a servant and a horse for me to ride, all of which served me well. For the first few days, I began to frequent her street, making rounds at all hours, but I could not see her. My constant rounds made certain people notice me, and then they had their eye on me. To throw these spies off track, I had to be more careful. My servant, in whom I had confided my love, counseled me, as he was older and more experienced. Carefully considering the situation,

[17] Gold coin stamped with two coats of arms on each side. At the end of the sixteenth century, the sum of 1,000 *doblados* (1,700,000 *maravedís*) was equivalent to what an average day laborer (who made approximately 85 *maravedís* a day) could only have made after 20,000 days of work. See the "Note on Coinage" in the introduction.

he suggested that, as my lord's house was undergoing repairs, I should purchase these work clothes and, changing my name so that no one would know who I was, I should settle down there as a stone worker. I considered what might happen to me if I carried out the plan, but since love and death conquer all, I overcame my own doubts, and it all seemed easy to me. I made up my mind, and it was the right choice. Then an unexpected thing happened: when the repairs were done, they kept me on as a gardener in that same house. That was truly my lucky day, and my moon grew full as I reached the pinnacle of my good fortune, for on the first day in my new position, and as soon as I set foot in the garden, I found myself before Daraja. I was no less surprised to see her than she was to see me. We gave each other an account of our lives, sharing with each other our misfortunes. She told me hers and I told her mine, and how my love for her friend had put me in such a state. I begged Daraja, as she knew full well who my parents were and who I was and of the noble blood of our line, to seek Elvira's favor for me, so that by her hand and generous intercession I might in holy matrimony enjoy the fruit of all my hopes. She promised to do so and fulfilled her promise as best she could. Yet my fortune is so miserly that, as soon as our tender love had finally begun to grow, the buds fell off, the flowers shriveled in a hot dry wind, and some worm gnawed at its roots so that it all came to an end. I was banished from their house with no explanation, falling from the pinnacle of good fortune to the lowest depth of despair. He that killed one bull with the stroke of a lance, he that killed the other in one blow of the sword, that was I, for I did it in her honor. She plainly saw me and recognized me, and was no end glad, as I read in her face and her eyes revealed to me. And if it were possible on this occasion, too, I would distinguish myself to please my lady and secure my everlasting fame by revealing who I am and what I am worth. I am ready to burst with grief at not being able to do so. If I could somehow manage it, I would give in exchange all the blood that runs through my veins. So you see, my lord, I have now given you a full account of my history and the whole sum of my misfortunes."

Don Alonso, having heard him out, threw his arms around him and held him tightly. Ozmín attempted to kiss his hands, but he would not allow it, saying: "These hands and arms are to be used in your service so that they might deserve to gain yours. This is no time for compliments, nor to alter your plans, until you wish to do so. As for the tournament, do not let it trouble you, for you shall enter the lists, no doubt about it."

Once again Ozmín attempted to kiss his hands, bending his knee to the ground. Don Alonso did the same, as they offered each other their support in the strength of their new friendship. Thus they passed in long conversation the days that remained until the tournament in which they were both to prove themselves.

I told you before how Don Rodrigo was secretly disliked for his arrogance. It seemed to Don Alonso that he had found what he sought, because if Jaime Vives were to joust in the tournament, he would surely defeat Don Rodrigo, humbling his pride. Ozmín, for his part, also longed to do so. And before it was time to arm himself, he walked slowly about in order to see Daraja come in, admiring how festive the plaza looked with its countless hangings of silk and gold, its varied colors, its curious windows, its beautiful ladies, their costumes and adornments, and the parade of illustrious people, so that all together it seemed like a priceless jewel with every detail a precious stone set within it. The tiltyard ran through the middle of the plaza, dividing it into two equal parts. The judges' scaffold was situated in a convenient spot and opposite the windows of Daraja and Doña Elvira. These two entered upon two white palfreys harnessed with trappings of silver and black velvet adornments, with great accompaniment. After having rounded the plaza, they took their seats. Once he saw Daraja there, Ozmín made his way out because the challengers were now about to enter. Shortly they arrived, wonderfully arrayed.

The shawms, trumpets, and other instruments began to play, strumming and sounding constantly until they had arrived at their places. Then the combatants entered, and among the first came Don Alonso, who, after his three very good courses (for few did better), returned home. He had already secured permission for a knight, a friend of his, whom he pretended to expect any moment from Jerez de la Frontera, to join the tournament, and Ozmín had been awaiting his return. They proceeded to the tiltyard together for Don Alonso served as his sponsor.

The Moor's arms were all black and so was his horse. He had no feathers in his helmet but instead a rose from Daraja's handkerchief, fashioned with great care—a clear sign by which she immediately recognized him. He took his place and, as luck had it, ran his first lance against one of the challenger's seconds. They gave the signal, and they raced off. Ozmín hit his adversary on the visor of his helmet, breaking his lance. Then he hit him again on a second pass with what remained of it, knocking him from the saddle to the ground over the haunches of his horse, yet the fall did him no more harm than what he suffered from the weight of the armor.

For Ozmín's last two courses, Don Rodrigo himself came forth. With his first lance, he grazed the Moor's left arm, while Ozmín wounded him on his right side, under his gardbrace, breaking his lance into three parts. With his last lance, Don Rodrigo missed, while Ozmín broke his on the beaver[18] of Don Rodrigo's helmet, leaving behind a large splinter of his lance. Everyone thought he had been badly hurt, but his helmet prevented him from being seriously harmed. Thus the Moor, having broken his three lances, was the proud victor. Even prouder was Don Alonso, who had sponsored him, and was beside himself with joy.

They left the plaza and went home to take off their arms without letting anyone recognize Ozmín. Then, wearing his ordinary dress, he left secretly by a small gate, returning to contemplate his Daraja and see what was happening in the tournament. He stood so close to the lady that they could almost have held hands. They looked at each other, yet his gaze was sad, and thus hers grew even sadder, wondering what could make it so that her sight did not cheer him. She did not know what to make of his jousting with weapons and a horse all in black, which is among them a bad omen.

All this caused her the most profound melancholy. It so took possession of her and weighed on her so heavily that no sooner were the festivities over when, her heart bursting in her chest, she left the window and hastened home. Those who were with her were surprised that

---

[18] Technical terms for parts of the armor: the gardbrace protects the upper arm, the beaver the nose and mouth.

nothing could cheer her. They gossiped about it, each one suspecting that which best suited his or her own malice. Don Luis, as a prudent knight, explained her behavior when he heard it questioned. And he did the same with his sons that night, saying to them:

"An afflicted soul weeps even among pleasures. What can possibly cheer one who is away from those she loves most? Good things are worth that much more when enjoyed in the company of those we know and consider our own. Delights may be found among strangers, but they are not deeply felt, and they increase the sorrow of a soul who sees in others a greater joy. I do not blame her nor am I surprised at her behavior; instead, I attribute it to her great prudence and strength, for the contrary would have reflected a blatant frivolity on her part. After all, she is away from her parents, far from her betrothed, and, although freely treated, a captive in a strange land, with no remedy for her troubles or any means to acquire it. Examine your own hearts and consider what it would mean to be in her place, and then you will feel what that is like. To do otherwise is to be like the healthy who urge the sick to eat and be well."

After this secret exchange, they publicly praised the knight from Jerez, exclaiming over how well he had jousted. And although they would have liked to know who he was, Don Alonso never said any more than what he had told them at first, and they believed it.

Meanwhile, Daraja's sadness increased day by day. Nobody could guess its cause, and they were all wide of the mark, although they took many stabs at it. They all came to the wrong conclusion, seeking to distract her as much as possible with whatever entertainments they could devise, yet no one was able to square the circle of her desires.

Don Luis had a house and an estate in Axarafe, a little village outside Seville. It was a temperate season, around February, a time of year when the game and the fields seem to come to life. They decided to pass a few days there at their leisure so as to leave no stone unturned in trying to distract Daraja from her sorrows. She seemed pleased at this development, assuming that if she left the city, she would find some way to see and speak to Ozmín. They prepared all the trappings for their expedition, and it was a happy sight to witness such commotion: one man led the greyhounds on their leashes; another brought the hounds and the ferret; others brought the falcons, another the owl;

some carried a gun on their shoulders or a crossbow in their hands; and others guided the loaded pack mules. They all traveled together with great noise and fanfare, rowdy with the excitement of the festivities.

Don Alonso had already heard the news, and he told Ozmín that their ladies had gone to the countryside for recreation and would be there for some time, with no word on when they would return. This was not all bad, they thought: in the country, they might have fewer rivals courting their ladies and more opportunities to go undetected.

The nights were neither clear nor too dark, neither cold nor hot, but delightfully calm and peacefully serene. The two enamored friends agreed to try their hand and their good luck by traveling to visit their ladies. Dressed as laborers, they left at sunset riding two nags. A quarter of a league before reaching the village, they dismounted near a country house, for on foot they would be less noticeable. Their plan would have succeeded had fortune not turned its back on them, for they arrived just when the ladies were out on a balcony, absorbed in conversation.

Don Alonso did not want to risk approaching them for fear of startling the quarry, and so asked his companion to sort things out by himself on behalf of them both, for as Doña Elvira loved him and Daraja knew him well, there was little to worry about. Thus Ozmín stole ahead little by little, nonchalantly singing in a low voice as if to himself an Arabic song, such that it would resound clearly for one who knew the language, but to one who did not and was not listening carefully, it would just sound like he was humming "la-la-la-la."

Doña Elvira said to Daraja: "Even these rude folk have their God-given gifts, if only they knew how to use them. Do you not hear that savage, what a sweet and tuneful voice he has, even though he is just humming nonsense? It's like the rain that falls on the sea, to no end."

"You know," Daraja said, "all things are esteemed according to the subject who possesses them. These laborers, if they are not transplanted into an urbane life while young, grafted from rough to cultivated soil, and stripped of that rugged bark in which they are born, will almost never learn good mores,[19] while on the contrary those who are

---

[19] The original uses the term *morigerados*: tempered or tamed. The verbal echo of *moro* (Moor) suggests Daraja's recognition that she speaks of Ozmín. Hence our choice of *mores*.

city dwellers and of a political nature are like the vine, which still gives fruit, although not much, even if neglected for a few years, and when well tended again responds in kind, brimming with the fruits of that labor. This man who sings here—not even a carpenter with his powerful axe and his adze would be able to straighten him out nor to make him useful. His cooing makes me sad. Let us go, if you please, for it is time for us to go to bed."

The two lovers had well understood each other—she, his song, and he, her words and to what end she spoke them. The ladies left, and Daraja lingered a little, asking him in Arabic to wait there. So he did, wandering up and down the street until she returned.

For some unknown reason, common folk always harbor a natural hatred for the noble sort, like the lizard for the snake, the swan for the eagle, the cock for the partridge, the prawn for the octopus, the dolphin for the whale, oil for pitch, the grapevine for the cabbage, and the like. And if you ask what might be the natural cause of this, no one knows more than that it is like the magnet that attracts steel, the heliotrope that follows the sun, the basilisk that kills with its glance, and the swallow-wort that helps the eyesight. Just as some things naturally love each other, others repel each other by celestial influence, the reason for which, to this day, men have not discerned. That things of different species should behave thus is no wonder because they have different constitutions, qualities, and natures. But rational men, the ones and the others molded from the same earth, of one flesh and blood, of one beginning and tending to the same end, of one law, of one religion, and all of them in every way self-same men! For all men naturally to love each other and for these to persist in their ways! That this stubborn rabble, more obdurate than Galician nuts, should persecute nobility with as much determination as they do never ceases to amaze me.

Some local lads were also out and about that night. They happened to see the strangers, and immediately, without any cause or reason and completely unprovoked, they called to each other and banded together, shouting, "Get the wolf! Get the wolf!" Tossing small stones at them like rain from the sky, they forced them to flee before any encounter. And so the two turned back, without even giving Ozmín a chance to say good-bye. They found their horses and rode back to the city, determined to return even later the next evening so that no one would hear them. Yet it was to no avail, for deathly lightning would not have made the villains leave their posts just so they might cause mischief and harm. They had barely set foot in the village the following night when a band of those louts formed around them, having recognized them. One with a slingshot, another with his arm, some with small lances, sticks, and spears, others with spits—leaving no shovels or oven mops behind, they set off after them as though they were chasing a rabid dog.

But they found the strangers better prepared than the night before for now the two wore sturdy armor, steel-plated helmets, and strong shields. From one side you could see stones, sticks, and shouts; from the other, strong sword strokes, and between the two, there was such commotion that the entire village appeared submerged in a fierce battle. As Don Alonso crossed a street unaware, they threw a stone at his chest with such force that he fell to the ground, unable to rejoin the fight. As best he could, he slowly backed away. Ozmín, meanwhile, drove them up the street, doing great damage to them, with not a few of them injured, and three dead.

As the commotion grew louder, the entire village came out at once. They blocked his way so that he could not escape, though he tried. From another direction, a clodhopper came up to him and gave him such a blow on the shoulder with the bar of a door that it brought him to his knees. Then not even the fact that he was the mayor's son could save him, for before he could strike again, Ozmín lunged at him and with one stroke of his sword split his head through the middle as though he were a kid goat, leaving him like a beached tuna on the shore, having paid with his life for his insolence. Then so many rushed at Ozmín with such force, from all directions, that he could no longer defend himself and so was made prisoner.

Daraja and Doña Elvira witnessed everything, from the beginning of the fray to the uproar as they captured him and tied his hands behind him with a rope, as if he were their equal. They all mistreated him in turn, punching, shoving, and kicking him, and ignominiously insulting him a thousand times over, taking their revenge on one who had surrendered. How shameful and ugly—only peasants such as these could act like this!

What do you make of this misfortune? And what can that lady have felt who worshipped Ozmín's very shadow? This, on the one hand, and on the other a number of dead and injured men, and her honor hung in the balance. For as soon as he learned of the case, Don Luis would be sure to ask what business Ambrosio had in the village. In her confusion, Daraja took counsel from necessity. She produced a letter, sealed it, and placed it in a little chest so that she could use it in her defense when Don Luis arrived.

By this time, daylight had come, and still the people had not settled down. They had sent to the city a report on the case so that an investigation could begin. Once the notary arrived, they began to examine witnesses. Many came forth unbidden, for evil people need no invitation to evil; it even makes enemies into friends. Some swore that there had been six or seven men with Ozmín; others that the strangers had come out of Don Luis's house and that from the window someone had yelled, "Kill them! Kill them!" Others claimed that the strangers had attacked the villagers, who had been calm and at peace, while yet others alleged that they been challenged in their own houses to come out and fight. And not one of them, though sworn to it, told the truth.

God deliver you from such peasants for they are as stiff as oaks and just as hard! They only yield their fruit when they are beaten and would rather be uprooted, destroyed completely, and their estates ravaged than bend a little. If they decide to persecute someone, they will perjure themselves a thousand times on what matters not a whit to them so long as they can cause harm. And what is worse: these wretches think that in this way they will save their souls, and it is a marvel if they confess to this venom.

The deaths and injuries were recorded, and the prisoner loaded with chains under careful watch. When Don Luis learned of it, he hastened to the village and inquired of his daughter, who told him what had actually happened. Then he asked Daraja, who said the same, adding that she had sent for Ambrosio so he could take a letter to Granada for her and that before he had even been able to speak to her, they had thrown stones at him two nights in a row; though her letter was written, she had been unable to send it.

Don Luis asked her to show him the letter to see what she might have to say, and she pretended to be reluctant to do so. Yet she was soon persuaded, as she actually wanted nothing else. Taking it from where she kept it, she said, "I give it to you so that my truth may be known, and so that no one may suspect that I write things that need to be kept secret."

Don Luis took it from her, but when he tried to read it, he saw that it was written in Arabic, and could not. So he found someone to read it to him: Daraja wrote to her father that she was concerned about his health and that she herself was well, and that other than for her desire to see him, she was more content and more pampered by Don Luis than any of his children. And so she beseeched her father that they should send Don Luis a gift in recognition of his courtesy and good hospitality.

When there are incidents such as these, words become heated, and people take their own assumptions about the matter as gospel; so they began gossiping about Don Luis and his household. This made Don Luis's hackles rise, but as a sensible knight, he thought it best to hide his feelings and return his household and family to the city.

When these events took place, Granada had already surrendered on the terms that we know from histories and that we still hear our parents relate. Among the nobles who remained in the city were the two fathers-in-law, Alboacén, who was Ozmín's father, and the mayor of Baza. Both asked for baptism, as they wanted to become Christians. Once this had been done, the mayor begged the King and Queen to give him license to see Daraja, his daughter. It was granted, and they said they would let him know how and when it would occur. Alboacén, who believed that his son was dead or captured, made many inquiries to try to find news of him but never discovered a trace. He was as afflicted as one might expect by the loss of such a son, the only heir of rich and noble parents. The mayor felt it no less, for he loved Ozmín as though he were his own son, and also for the grief Daraja would feel when they gave her such dire news.

The King and Queen, for their part, sent a messenger to Seville to request Don Luis to come to them from wherever he was and bring

Daraja with him, with all due respect, as they had entrusted her to him. When these letters were received and the order understood, Daraja was beside herself: it meant she would have to leave without knowing how things would turn out or in how tight a situation she was leaving the prisoner.

She found herself distracted, pensive, and dejected, deeming herself a thousand times more unfortunate than misfortune itself and the most injured of all women. She longed to sweep everything aside and lose her life alongside her husband. In her doubt, she almost decided on a most atrocious error, a sign of the chaste and true love that she felt for Ozmín. But her good judgment allowed her to cast her cruel thoughts aside; she returned to her good senses and determined to leave her misfortunes in the hands of Fortune, her enemy, and to await whatever end she might give them. Since death was the utmost evil, she would not take her own life. But the barrier of her long suffering could not contain the sea of tears that burst from her eyes. Everyone assumed that they were for the happiness of returning to her family, and they were all deceived. They all encouraged her, and yet no one could console her.

Don Rodrigo arrived to bid her farewell. With her cheeks bathed in the crystal streams that dropped from her divine eyes, she said to him: "I hope to persuade you, lord Don Rodrigo, with an abundance of reasons to do the favor that I need to ask of you at this moment. It is so just that neither can I refrain from asking nor you from granting it to me for it so concerns you. You already know how obliged we are to do good where required, as this is a divine natural law that touches everyone and which no savage ignores. This law becomes stronger the more reasons are added to it, and among these, a key and not insignificant one is the obligation we incur to those who have served us.[20] This alone should be enough that, given who you are, I should not even need to intercede. But what I want to ask of you, given this obligation, is as follows. As you know, Ambrosio served both your parents and my own. We are bound to help him, and I all the more so, for the sentence

---

[20] The original states "our obligation to those to whom we have given our bread," emphasizing the responsibility of the noble person for those of his or her household.

he presently endures is all my fault and his only concern in the matter was my own interest. I placed him in danger, a responsibility that I must assume. If you wish to free me from this burden, if you have ever longed to please me, if you want to place me in your debt so that I shall remain forever grateful, then you must procure his liberty, which is also mine, as earnestly as I beseech you. My lord Don Luis, before he leaves me here, will do everything he can through his friends and relatives so that all might come together in his absence to deliver me from this obligation. . . ."

Don Rodrigo promised her to do so, and thus they parted. The poor lady left her beloved husband in such danger and suffered for him more and more the farther she traveled from him, so that by the time she reached Granada she did not seem like herself. They took her immediately to the palace, where we must leave her and return to the prisoner, whom Don Rodrigo assisted as though he had been his own brother.

Don Alonso, who had fled the brawl with injuries to his chest, had taken to his bed in a bad state. When he learned that the prisoner had been brought to Seville, however, he got up and tirelessly pursued the case as though it had been his own. But all the parties made their accusations, the plaintiffs were full of ill will, and the dead and injured were many so that they could not prevent Ozmín's being sentenced to hang in public.

Don Rodrigo was furious at such a show of disrespect toward him and his father as to attempt to hang their innocent servant. Don Alonso, for his part, insisted that a knight of noble blood, such as his friend Jaime Vives, could not be hanged. Even had his crime been greater, the difference between the persons should spare him his life and especially such a death as hanging; he should instead be beheaded.

The judges were confused, unsure of what was the case. Don Rodrigo calls him a servant and Don Alonso a friend; Don Rodrigo defends him as Ambrosio, while Don Alonso pleads for Jaime Vives, a knight from Zaragoza, who at the bullfight had carried out the two feats that the entire city had witnessed, and at the joust, for which Don Alonso had sponsored him, had defeated the challenger, valiantly proving himself. The difference was so pronounced, the names so contradictory, and their alleged qualities so discrepant that in order to resolve these doubts the judges decided to take Ozmín's own declaration.

They asked him if he was a knight. He responded that he was noble and of royal blood, but that his name was neither Ambrosio nor Jaime Vives. They asked him to give his name and some account of his person. He answered that revealing who he was would not prevent the punishment, and that if he was to die regardless, it was as unnecessary for him to say and that it did not matter whether he suffered one form of death or another. They begged him to say if he was the one that Don Alonso claimed, who had so distinguished himself at the bullfight and the joust. He answered that it had been him but that his name was not what they had claimed.

Because he refused so vehemently to identify himself, they assumed he was a nobleman. And so they took some time trying to confirm who he was, why the two knights defended him so, and, moreover, why the whole city longed for his freedom and was so taken with him. So they sent a messenger to Zaragoza to find out the truth of the matter and his actual origins, yet after a few days and many inquiries, they had discovered no one who could tell them about him or knew who a knight of such a name and appearance might be. When they returned with this bad news, his friends begged him and the judges required him over and over again to identify himself, but he did not wish to do so, nor was it possible. After this respite, the judges, much against their will and pitying his youth and valor, could not refrain from executing justice as the plaintiffs insistently demanded, and so they confirmed their sentence.

Neither Daraja nor her parents had a moment's rest while this was occurring, as they had already relayed an account of the entire case to their Royal Highnesses, who were now informed of the truth. They submitted petition after petition. Daraja personally pleaded for her husband's life as a special boon but received no response. Yet soon Don Luis was secretly dispatched with a royal order to the judges that, no matter what stage Ozmín's case had reached, the entire thing from the start should be delivered unto the monarchs along with the prisoner in order to do them service.

Don Luis left posthaste, as he was instructed, while poor Daraja, her father, and her father-in-law broke down in tears at the thought of how quickly the judges might dispatch the poor knight and how slow the response to their petitions and pleas for mercy had been. They knew not what to make of such a delay, during which no one gave them any positive or negative response or any reason to hope. This caused them much grief, and they could not find a solution, even though they never stopped trying, as they feared above all the danger of the delay.

While they wondered what to do, Don Luis—as I said—was already swiftly and very secretly on his way. As he entered the gates of Seville, Ozmín was exiting the gates of the jail to be executed. The streets and plazas through which they took him were full of people and the entire city in an uproar. There was not one person whose eyes were dry at the sight of such a fine and handsome young man, brave and well loved for the famous feats he had publicly performed, and what made them saddest was that he refused to confess before dying. They all thought he did it for a chance to escape or to prolong his life a little. Yet he spoke not a word, nor showed any sadness on his face; instead he gazed upon them all as he passed, almost with a smile on his face. They stopped him and tried to persuade him to confess so that he might not lose his soul along with his body, but he would not answer and kept silent through it all.

While they were all in this state of confusion, with the whole city awaiting the sad spectacle, Don Luis arrived, pressing his way through the crowd to stop the execution. The bailiffs thought he was resisting justice, but because they feared him greatly and he was a bold and powerful knight, they abandoned Ozmín and with great commotion hastened to tell their superiors what had happened. These, in turn, came to inquire what might account for such disrespect for the rule of law. Don Luis came to meet them with the prisoner in hand. He showed them the order and message from the King and Queen, which they obeyed with great pleasure. Then to everyone's delight, and with all the knights of that city in attendance, they took Ozmín to Don Luis's house, turning that night into an elegant masquerade, with torches and lamps lit in the streets and windows to show the general happiness. To celebrate, they longed to hold public festivities in the days following because they had by then discovered who he was. Yet Don Luis gave them no time for, as had been instructed, he left with the prisoner the very next morning, transporting him in a most comfortable manner.

Once they had arrived in Granada, he held him secretly for a few days until their Royal Highnesses ordered him to take Ozmín to the palace. When he was brought to them, they were delighted to see him, and with him before them, they sent for Daraja to come out. When they saw each other in such a place as that, completely unbeknownst to one another, you may judge with your own hearts the unforeseen happiness they experienced and what they each felt. The Queen went toward them and announced that their fathers had become Christians, although Daraja already knew it. She asked whether they would do so as well, promising them great rewards, but said that no love nor fear should oblige them save that of God and their own salvation because either way, from that moment on, they were free to do as they wished with their persons and their estates.

Ozmín wanted to answer with all the joints and sinews of his body, turning them into so many tongues to give thanks for such great mercy. He stated that he wished to be baptized, and before the King and Queen he asked his wife to do the same. Daraja, whose eyes, brimming with soft tears, had not left her husband, then cast them toward the King and Queen. Because it had been the divine will to reveal to them the true light, leading them to it through such harsh trials, she said, she was ready with all her heart to do the same and to swear obedience to the King and Queen, her lords, in whose care and royal hands she placed herself.

And so they were baptized: he was christened Ferdinand and she Isabella, after their Royal Highnesses, who served as their godparents for both their baptism and their wedding just a few days later, granting them many favors in that city, where they lived and had an illustrious lineage.

※　※

We had listened to that story in complete silence for the whole way, until we arrived within view of Cazalla. The priest seemed to have timed it perfectly, even though he told it to us at greater length and with a different soul than I have recounted it here.

Part II

Contexts

──────────── ✠ Moorish Ballads ✠ ────────────

The long tradition of folk ballads about Christian-Moorish relations in Iberia was transformed in the late sixteenth century by the *romancero morisco*, a new generation of printed and authored ballads, penned by well-known writers, quickly anthologized, and hugely popular. Tremendously popular in its own right, "The Abencerraje" also contributed to this new form, providing material for a large number of ballads, including one by the famous playwright Lope de Vega, a fragment of which is translated below.

The fascination with Moorish ballads was so widespread and intense in this period that some poets resented the idealization of Spain's ostensible enemies. In their verse criticism, of which we reproduce two brief examples below, they argued that Spanish poets and readers should stick to Spanish concerns and abandon the "exotic" topoi of the maurophile ballads. If poets needed to disguise any real people in their characters, they should turn to properly Spanish alter egos, such as shepherds, and avoid the ubiquitous Moors. A fascinating response emerged, however, also in ballad form, as other poets argued that Moorish topoi were very much Spanish and thus a most fitting subject for Spanish ballads. In translating the ballads, we have preserved the "Moorish" terms, to give a flavor of how this vocabulary saturated them.

✠ I ✠

Celindo came to Cártama[1]
With your letter in that season
When the sun was in the South,
Sad and opaque, for good reason.
I read it, kissed it and placed within it
All my hopes of being there,
Hope later lost in an absence

That left it full of greying hairs.
I dressed, oh lovely lady,
In colors, finery, and feathers
For the joy that was in my heart
In all three of them is declared.
I went down to our former orchard
And said good-bye out loud
To the trees and to the flowers,
To the waters and the founts.
I gave them a thousand embraces;
They also were so inclined,
Giving me their caresses for you
For plants have souls of this kind.
I set my feet on the stirrups
Without the saddlebow,
And turning back to the house,
I said to it what follows:
"Stones, Jarifa awaits me."
I know not if they answered,
But for a long time thereafter
The fountains all resounded,
Full envious or in praise of you.

▣ II ▣

So much Zaida and Adalifa,[2]
So much Draguta and Darafa,
So much Azarque, so much Adulce,
So much Gazul and Abenámar;
So much *alquicer* and *marlota*,
So much *almaizar* and *almalafa*,
So many devices and feathers,
So many medals and ciphers,
So much trade in Moorish clothing,
Banderillas, shields, and all
Covered in mottos and matter,

As far as the eye can see—
They will be the death of me!

▨ III ▨

Oh, my honored poets,[3]
Uncover your faces at once!
Let those Moors take off their finery,
Put an end to all those *zambras*.[4]
Let Gazul go with God,
And the devil take Celindaja,
Return those *marlotas*
To those from whom you had them.
You neglect a strong Bernardo,
Living glory of our Spain,
You disdain a warring Cid,
A Diego Ordóñez de Lara.[5]
Instead, your songs of the cicada
Celebrate the Moorish rabble!
If any names must be hidden,
Because circumstances demand it,
Could you not instead find them
In the woods and huts of the rustics?

▨ IV ▨

What good is it for Gazul[6]
To strike another with his lance,
When today a Lethean nymph[7]
Wants to undo all his *zambras*?
It is not as if Don Pedro were
More honorable than Amenábar,
 Or Doña María were better
Than the beautiful Celindaxa.
If Don Rodrigo is Spanish,
Spanish is the strong Audalla,

[95]

And my lord Mayor should know
That so is Guadalara.
If Doña Juana when she pleases
Dances a Spanish *gallarda*,[8]
The *zambras* are all that too,
For Spain is Granada.

NOTES

1 This ballad was included in Lope's 1596 play *El remedio en la desdicha* and is translated here from the version reproduced in Francisco López Estrada, *El Abencerraje (novela y romancero)*, 180–83.

2 The original ballad is reproduced in Agustín Durán, ed., *Romancero general*, vol. 10, p. 128, n. 244. The italicized terms in this ballad refer to Moorish items of clothing. The names themselves come from Arabic. The *alquicer* is a cloak (often made of white wool); the *marlota* is a tight tunic or cloak; the *almaizar* is a head wrap made of fine soft fabric; and the *almalafa* is a cloak that drapes from the shoulders to the feet (*Diccionario de la Real Academia española*). Although the ballad makes them seem exotic, many of these items were also worn by Christians, especially for such occasions as the *juegos de cañas*.

3 The original ballad is reproduced in Durán, 129, n. 245.

4 *Zambra* refers to a festive occasion with music and dancing. The name comes from Arabic.

5 Bernardo, the Cid, and Diego Ordóñez de Lara are all heroes of medieval Spanish lore.

6 The original ballad is reproduced in Durán, 129–30, n. 246.

7 The classicizing nymph provides an alternative to the Moorish topoi of the ballad. In Greek mythology, the underworld river Lethe was associated with oblivion and the erasure of memory.

8 A *gallarda* is a type of dance.

From *Civil Wars of Granada*

GINÉS PÉREZ DE HITA

Pérez de Hita was a master shoemaker and occasional writer of religious pageants in the city of Murcia, in southern Spain. His fictionalized account of the last days of the Nasrid court in Granada, full of jousts, combats, and love affairs, proved wildly popular in a Spain that craved stories of idealized Moors. As an early historical novel, the first part of the *Civil Wars* (1595) was also a hugely influential literary model within Spain and beyond, expanding on the single idealized Moor of "The Abencerraje" to render an entire court. Pérez de Hita invented an Arabic source for his text, claiming that it was taken from an Arabic book by one "Aben Hamin, native of Granada" and that he had merely translated it, a device that Cervantes would reuse to great effect in *Don Quixote* (1605). Pérez de Hita also included hugely popular Moorish ballads within his text, often—and to our eyes quite paradoxically—as proof of the historical truth of the events he relates.

A far more controversial second part of the *Civil Wars*, a first-person account of the 1568 uprising of the Moriscos in the Alpujarras, in which Pérez de Hita had participated, was not published until 1604. By yoking together both moments as "civil wars of Granada," Pérez de Hita emphasizes the continuity between the noble Moors idealized in his first part and the oppressed Moriscos whose uprising he chronicles in the second. In this excerpt from Part I, Pérez de Hita narrates the violent rivalry between the Abencerrajes and other noble clans in Granada, and their destruction at the hand of the jealous king Abū 'Abd Allah, often known as the Small King or Boabdil. Discomfited after a failed raid on Jaén, the king is predisposed to think ill of his bravest knights. Note that this is the backstory of Abindarráez's family, as he alludes to it in "The Abencerraje."

⊞ ⊞

The Small King of Granada was in the Alijares,[1] as we mentioned ear-lier. One of the Zegrí knights proposed that the knights of Jaén were braver than the Abencerrajes because they had forced them to retreat against their will. The King responded, "That may well be, but were it not for the bravery of the Abencerraje and Alabez knights, none of us would have made it back to Granada. They acted so bravely that we all managed to escape, without losing the cattle and the captives that we had brought with us from our raid."

"Oh, how blind you are, Your Majesty," exclaimed the Zegrí knight. "How you defend those traitors to the Royal Crown! You are too kind and trusting by far to the Abencerrajes, unaware of the treason they have been plotting against you. There are many knights in Granada who have wanted to say something to you but have not dared, knowing how much you credit their lineage. In truth, I would prefer not to say anything, but I am bound to protect the honor of my lord and king. So I warn Your Majesty that from this day on you must never again, in any fashion, trust any Abencerraje knight, if you do not wish to lose your kingdom."

Troubled, the King responded, "My friend, tell me what it is you know. Do not hide it from me, and I will promise you great favors."

"Would I were not the one to reveal this secret but that it were someone else! Yet I will speak because Your Majesty orders me to do so, as long as you give me your royal word not to give me away. For Your Majesty knows full well that I and all those of my line are not in the Abencerrajes' good graces so that they might say that we have set Your Majesty against them out of envy of their nobility, good fortune, and fame, and I would not want this for the world."

"Do not concern yourself over such a matter," said the King. "I give you my royal word that no one will hear it from me, nor will I reveal it."

"In that case, Your Majesty should send for Mahandín Gomel, who also knows this secret, and my two nephews Mahomad and Alhamuy, for they are all such noble knights that they would never let me speak falsely about what they have seen, along with four other Gomel knights, cousins of the said Mahandín Gomel."

The King, no longer at ease, sent for them. Once they had all been brought to him in secret, with no other knights present, the Zegrí knight began to speak, with a great show of reluctance: "You must know, powerful king, that all the Abencerraje knights are plotting to kill you in order to take your kingdom. They are grown insolent because my lady the Queen is the lover of the Abencerraje Albinhamad, one of the richest and most powerful knights in Granada. What can I say, oh, King of Granada, except that every Abencerraje thinks himself a king, a lord, a prince. There is no one in Granada who does not adore them—they are more beloved than Your Majesty himself. Well you must remember, my lord, when we held festivities in the Generalife and the Grand Master of Arms called for a duel, in which it was Muza's lot to face him.[2] That day, as Gomel, the knight here before us, and I were strolling through the garden of the Generalife, down one of the myrtle lanes, I suddenly spied the Queen underneath a huge white rose bush, taking her pleasure with Albinhamad. So sweetly did they dally that they did not hear us. I showed this to Mahandín Gomel, who is present here, and who would not let me lie about it. Quietly we left the scene and waited to see what would happen. After a short while, we saw the Queen come out by herself, down near the laurel fountain and bit by bit, reservedly, join her ladies-in-waiting. A long while after, we saw Albinhamad leave very slowly, dissembling, circling the garden and picking white and red roses to make a crown that he placed on his head. We went toward him as though we knew nothing and asked him what he had been doing. Albinhamad answered, 'I have been taking pleasure in this garden, which is so rich and has so much to see.' Saying this, he gave us each two roses, and so we talked as we walked to where Your Majesty was with all the other knights. We wanted to let you know what had happened, but we dared not as it was such a grave matter, and so as not to defame the Queen and unsettle your court, for you were then still a new king. This is what is going on—open your eyes and look that you do not lose your kingdom and then your life, which matters most, as you have already lost your honor. Is it possible that you have never noticed or perceived what the Abencerrajes are after? Do you not recall, during the ring game, the royal float that the Abencerrajes offered? Remember how on the ram on its prow there was a globe made of glass and around it letters that spelled, 'Everything is too little'? So they express that the world is not enough for them.[3] And on top, above the highest lantern of the float, they showed a savage breaking the jaws of a lion. What could that mean but that you are the lion and they are the ones who kill you and finish you off? Come to your senses, my lord, and inflict a punishment to astound the world. Let the Abencerrajes die and with them the immoderate and adulterous Queen, for dragging your honor through the mud in this way."

The King felt such shame and sorrow upon hearing the treacherous Zegrí's story that, crediting it, he fell to the floor as if dead for a long time. When he returned to his senses, he opened his eyes and let out a deep sigh, saying, "Oh, Mohammed! How have I offended you? Is this your repayment for all the goods and service that I have offered you, for the sacrifices I have made to you, for the mosques I have had built in your name, for the copious incense I have burned at your altars? Oh, traitor, how you have betrayed me. No more traitors—by Allah, the Abencerrajes shall perish, and the Queen shall be burned to death. Come, my knights, we shall go to Granada, and let the Queen be arrested at once. I shall exact a punishment that will be heard around the world."

One of the treacherous knights, a Gomel, replied, "Not like this, for you will not succeed. If you arrest the Queen, all will be lost, and you will risk your life and kingdom. For if the Queen is captured, Albinhamad will immediately guess the cause of her imprisonment and will suspect something. He will enlist all of his line to prepare to attack you and defend the Queen. And even beyond that, you already know that the Alabeces, Vanegas, and Gazules are of their band and are partial to them, and all of them the best of Granada. What you should do to avenge yourself is to send for the Abencerrajes to come to your royal palace one by one, very secretly and without any commotion. And you should have with you twenty or thirty well-armed knights whom you trust, and as each Abencerraje knight comes in, you shall order that his throat be cut. If you do this one by one, by the time the case is revealed, not a single one of them will be left. When their friends hear of it and set out to harm you, you will already have intimidated the kingdom and will have all the Zegrí, Gomel, and Maza knights on your side.

These are not so few nor do they fight so poorly that they would not lead you to peace and save you from all harm. Once this is done, you shall send for the Queen to be arrested, and you will bring her case to justice, accusing her of adultery. Then, you will announce that the four knights who accuse her shall fight against four knights who defend her. If those who defend her beat the accusers, the Queen shall be set free, but if the knights on her side are defeated, then the Queen shall die. And so all who are of the Queen's line, along with the Almoradís, the Almohades, and the Marines, will not prove so stubborn, nor will they make a move without thinking about it, knowing that justice is on your side, and they will be satisfied. Leave the rest to us, my lord, for we will arrange matters so that you are avenged and your life and kingdom secured.

"You advise me well, my loyal knights," said the King. "But who are the four knights who shall accuse the Queen and battle for her? Let them be such that they may succeed in their suit."

"Do not worry about that, Your Majesty," said the treacherous Zegrí, "for I will be one of them, my cousin Mahardón another, Mahandín the third, and his brother Alyhamete the fourth. Trust in Mohammed, for in all your court there are no four other knights so brave or so strong, even if you take Muza into account."

"Let us go, then," said the deceived and unlucky king. "Let it be done thus. We shall go to Granada and give orders to take just revenge. Oh, Granada, how unlucky you are, and what a turn you face! How great shall be your fall so that you shall never be able to rise again, nor recover your nobility or your wealth!"

With this, the traitors and the King headed to Granada, and upon entering the Alhambra, they went to the royal residence. The Queen and her ladies-in-waiting came out to the palace gates to greet them. Yet the King did not wish to look upon the Queen and instead walked by without lingering with her as was his habit. The Queen, bewildered by this behavior and with no idea of what caused such unusual disdain from the King, took to her chambers with her ladies. The King, dissembling, spent the whole day with his knights until evening, when he dined early and retired to his chamber, claiming that he felt ill. All the knights retired to their lodgings. The unlucky King spent the night preoccupied by a thousand thoughts; he could not rest. He said to himself: "Oh, unfortunate Audillí, king of Granada, how close you are to losing yourself and your kingdom. If I kill these knights, great harm will come to me and my kingdom. Yet if I do not kill them and what I have been told is true, I am also lost. I know not what remedy might deliver me from these tribulations! Is it possible that knights of such illustrious lineage should think on such treason? I cannot persuade myself that it should be so. Is it possible that my wife, the Queen, should commit such evil? I do not believe it because I have never seen in her anything that does not befit an honest woman. But what purpose, what cause would lead the Zegríes to tell me this? It is a mystery why they have told me. If it is true, by Allah the all-powerful, the Abencerrajes and the Queen shall die."

The King spent all night ruminating on this and other various thoughts, with no sleep, until in the morning he rose from bed and went out to his royal palace, where he found many knights waiting for him. They were all Zegríes, Gomeles, and Mazas, and with them all the treacherous knights. They all rose from their seats and showed great respect to the King, wishing him good morning. Meanwhile, a squire came in to tell the King that the night before, Muza and the Abencerraje knights had arrived from the Vega, where they had been fighting Christians, and that they had brought with them two vanquished Christian standards and more than twenty heads.[4] The king appeared to be delighted by the news as he had no choice. Calling aside the treacherous Zegrí, he ordered him to station thirty well-armed knights in the Court of the Lions and to have the executioner ready with everything necessary to carry out what they had discussed. The traitor Zegrí left the royal palace at once to execute the King's orders.

Once everything was ready, the King was notified and went to the Court of the Lions, where he found the treacherous Zegrí with thirty Zegrí and Gomel knights, all of them well armed and with them an executioner. At once he sent his page to summon Abencarrax, his high constable. The page bid him come on behalf of the King. Abencarrax heeded the royal call, and as soon as he entered the Court of the Lions, they captured him without any chance for him to resist. At once his throat was slit over a large alabaster bowl. Albinhamad, who had been accused of committing adultery with the Queen, was then called to the same fate, and his throat was cut like that of the first knight. In this way did thirty-six Abencerraje knights, the most illustrious in Granada, have their throats slit without anyone knowing. They might all have been killed, with not a single one surviving, but that God our Savior came to their aid, for their works and bravery in life did not merit such a lowly end as they had been good friends to Christians and had done them good favors. Some who were present when their throats were slit even say that the Abencerrajes died as Christians, calling on the crucified Christ to assist them and show them favor in their moment of peril. So it was later said.[5]

To return to the matter at hand: God did not want such cruelty to go any further. And so a young page of these Abencerraje knights went in with his lord, without anyone noticing him. He witnessed how they slit his lord's throat, and he saw the other murdered knights whom he knew full well. When they opened the door to call in another knight, the young page escaped. Full of fear and weeping for his lord, he came across the knights Malique Alabez, Abenámar, and Sarrazino near the Alhambra fountain, where the line of trees is today. They were all going up to the Alhambra to speak with the King. Shaking and overcome by sobs, the page warned them: "Oh, noble knights, in Allah's holy name, do not go any further or you will die a horrible death!"

"What do you mean?" answered Alabez.

"My lord," said the page, "Know that in the Court of the Lions there lie a great number of murdered knights, all Abencerrajes, and my lord among them. I saw them slit his throat, for I went with him into the Court and they did not notice me because holy Allah wished it so. When they opened the false door to the Court again, I fled. By Mahommed's holy name, you must believe this."

The three Moorish knights were bewildered and looked at each other without knowing what to say or whether to believe what they had heard.

Abenámar said, "If this is true, there is great treason here, upon my life!"

"How shall we find out?" Sarrazino inquired.

"I will tell you how," said Alabez. "Stay here, my lords, and if you see any knight going up to the Alhambra, whether Abencerraje or not, do not let him pass. Tell them to wait a while, and in the meantime I will go to the royal residence to find out what is happening. I'll return shortly.

"May Allah guide you," Abenámar said. "We shall await you here."

The Malique knight quickly went up to the Alhambra, and as he went in the gate, he came across the King's page, who was heading out in a great rush. The Malique knight asked him, "Where to in such a hurry?"

"I am off to call an Abencerraje knight," the page replied.

"On whose behalf?" the Malique knight inquired.

"On behalf of my lord the King," the page responded. "Do not hold me back for I cannot stop. Yet if you, lord Malique, want to do a good deed, go down to the city and tell any Abencerrajes you find that they should leave Granada immediately because there is great evil afoot against them."

So saying, the page hurried off, rushing to the city.

The valiant Malique Alabez, now satisfied and certain that there was some great evil afoot, returned to where he had left Sarrazino and the good Abenámar. "Good friends," he told them, "there is certainly a great plot against the Abencerraje knights. The king's page, whom you might have seen pass by, asked me to tell all the Abencerrajes that I find that they should leave the city for there is great evil afoot against them."

"By Allah," exclaimed Sarrazino, "may I be struck down if the Zegríes are not behind this! Let us leave at once for the city and warn of what is going on so that such great evil may be remedied."

"Let us go," said Abenámar, "for we must not be remiss in this matter."

With these words, the three returned to the city in a great hurry. Before they reached the street of the Gomeles, they came across Captain Muza with more than twenty Abencerraje knights of those who had gone to the Vega to fight the Christians. They were on their way to see the King and tell him of their expedition. As soon as he saw them, Alabez exclaimed excitedly, "Knights, prepare yourselves, for there is a great treachery against you! The King has had more than thirty knights of your line killed."

Shocked and frightened, the Abencerrajes did not know what to say, but the brave Muza said to them, "By my faith as a knight, if there is treachery afoot, then the Zegríes and the Gomeles must be part of it, for I have noticed that they are nowhere to be seen in the city. They must all be at the Alhambra with the King."

He turned around and declared, "Come with me, all of you, for I will solve this."

So they all returned to the city with the brave Muza. When they arrived at the Plaza Nueva, Muza, as military commander, immediately sent for a bugler. As soon as he appeared, Muza ordered him to sound a call to arms. The bugler followed orders, and as soon as they heard him, men began to gather, with some arriving on horseback and others on foot, including the captains who were standard-bearers and the soldiers. Many great knights, among the most illustrious in Granada, gathered there. The only ones missing were the Zegríes, the Gomeles, and the Mazas, which confirmed the suspicion that the Zegríes were responsible for the conspiracy. When all these men had gathered, the courageous Malique Alabez, whose heart beat as if it were outside his body, began to shout: "Brave knights and citizens here today, know that there has been great treason done, and that the Small King has ordered a great number of the Abencerraje knights to be killed. If the conspiracy had not been revealed by the will of holy Allah, none would be alive now. Let us all seek vengeance: we do not want a tyrannous king who kills in this manner the knights who defend his land."

Malique Alabez had barely finished when the whole mob of commoners began to shout and cry out, rallying the city as they cried: "Treason! Treason! The King has killed the Abencerraje knights! Death to the King! Death to the King! We do not want a treasonous King!"

This shouting and commotion began to spread throughout Granada with a diabolic furor. They all took arms and began to head up to the Alhambra. At a moment's notice, more than forty thousand men—citizens, officials, merchants, commoners, and other sorts of people—had come together. It was an impressive and awesome sight to see so many men gather so quickly, without even counting the knights on horseback who gathered also. There were the remaining Abencerrajes, of whom there were over two hundred knights, and along with them the Gazules, Vanegas, Alabeces, Almoradís, Almohades, Azarques, and all the other lines of knights of Granada. They all shouted, "If this is allowed, then some other day they will kill another line among those that yet remain." The shouting and the noise were tremendous, and the confusing conflict deafened all of Granada. From far away one could hear the shouting of men, the screaming of women, and the crying of children. It seemed as though the world were ending, and the noise could clearly be heard in the Alhambra. Guessing what it was, the fearful King ordered the gates to the Alhambra to be closed. He began to realize what bad advice he had followed in what he had done and was amazed to learn that the secret had been revealed.

The great crowd and confusion of people reached the Alhambra, yelling and shouting, "Death to the King! Death to the King!" When they found the gates locked, they quickly called for fire to burn them down, which was soon done. In four or six different places, they set fire to the Alhambra, with such force and violence that it quickly began to burn. King Muley Hacén, father of the Small King, heard the great revolt and commotion, having already been notified of its cause. He was very angry at the King, his son, and hoped that he would be killed, so he ordered a secret gate to the Alhambra to be opened at once with the excuse that he wanted to go out and quiet the disturbance. But as soon as the gate was opened, a thousand men were ready to press in.

Recognizing the old King, they rushed to him and lifted him in the air, shouting,

"This is our King, and no other! Long live the old King Muley Hacén!"

Leaving him well guarded, a great number of knights and foot soldiers entered through the false gate. They were Gazules, Alabeces, and Abencerrajes, along with some foot soldiers, who numbered over two hundred.

The old King quickly closed the false gate, ordering many who had remained with him to defend it so that no more harm would be done within the Alhambra than what those already inside might do. But this effort was in vain as those already inside were enough to destroy a hundred Alhambras. The others ran through the streets screaming, "Death to the King and the rest of the traitors!" Violently they came to the royal residence, where they found only the Queen and her ladies as though dead, with no idea what had caused the disturbance and such unforeseen events. When they asked where the bad King was, they did not lack for one to tell them that he was in the Court of the Lions. Then the entire host went in that direction and found the doors locked with strong bolts. Yet the defenses were useless as the crowd broke the bolts to pieces and went into the chamber, despite the many Zegrí knights who guarded the entrance. When the Abencerraje, Gazul, and Alabez knights entered, they saw in that courtyard the slaughter of the Abencerraje knights, which the king had ordered. Who could describe the rage and fury that this cruel spectacle ignited in the living Abencerrajes as in all those who came with them? Fiercer than any tiger, they turned on the more than five hundred Zegrí, Gomel, and Maza knights who were in that vast and wide courtyard to defend the Small King, shouting, "Death to the traitors who have perpetrated and advocated this treason!" Then they furiously attacked them, slashing and stabbing them.

The Zegríes and those on their side defended themselves strongly because they were well armed and ready for the encounter. Yet their readiness did not avail them for they were torn to pieces—in less than an hour, a great number of Zegrí, Gomel, and Maza knights had been killed. Determined in their attack, their opponents continued to kill and injure many more. Great noise and commotion reigned as the men who had come from the city pressed close, shouting constantly, "Death to the King and to the traitors!" Such was the destruction wrought by the Abencerraje, Alabez, and Gazul knights, and so great was their revenge for the dead Abencerrajes, that of all the Zegríes, Gomeles, and Mazas who were there, very few were left alive. The unlucky King hid and could not be found. At this point, the knights who had been treacherously killed, who were thirty-six of the richest and most illustrious, were taken down to the city. There, in the Plaza Nueva, they were placed on black poles so that the entire city could see them and be moved to compassion by such a doleful and sad spectacle, so full of cruelty. The rest of the men ransacked the Alhambra, looking for the King with such fury that all the towers and houses there crumbled, so that the sounds of destruction echoed across the mountains. If the Alhambra was full of tumult and noise, no less uproar and crying came from the unfortunate city. All the people together mourned the dead Abencerrajes. Certain houses mourned the deaths of the Zegríes, Gomeles, and Mazas, and of other knights who died near them in the riot. And because of this ill-fated conflict and uproar the following ballad was recited, which begins and goes like this:

> In the towers of the Alhambra
> a great shouting was heard
> as the city of Granada
> was with weeping stirred;
> for the King, for no reason,
> in one day had murdered
> thirty-six Abencerrajes,
> worthy knights, fine to see,
> whom Zegríes and Gomeles
> accused of treachery.
> Granada cries for them,
> Oh what sorrow it feels!
> In losing such knights
> they lost much indeed.
> Men, women, and children
> mourn this tremendous fall,
> the ladies of Granada,
> mourn them one and all.
> The streets and the windows
> are all covered in black,
> black wear knights and ladies,
> for those who won't come back.
> Gomeles, full treacherous
> alone do not mourn
> and with them the Zegríes
> who helped them in turn.

For Gazules and Alabeces
They mourn only, in short,
in revenge for excesses,
killed in the Lion Court.
And were the king to be found,
they would soon take his life,
for allowing the malice
that caused so much strife.

To return now to the bloody and long-lasting riot of the Granadan people against the Small King and his protectors, it must be said that the valiant Muza, as soon as he saw the Alhambra set on fire, quickly began to put out the furious flames. He knew that the King Muley Hacén, his father, had ordered the false gate to the Alhambra to be opened, and so he came through that same gate with a great number of knights and foot soldiers. Once inside, he found the King Muley Hacén with more than a thousand knights to defend him, and they all shouted: "Long live King Muley Hacén, whom we take as our lord, and not the Small King, who has so viciously killed the best knights of Granada!"

Muza responded, "Long live King Muley Hacén, my father! For that is what all Granada wants!"

All those who were with Muza echoed his words, and so they entered the Alhambra and went straight to the royal residence. Although they searched it up and down, they could not find the King. Amazed, they turned to the Court of the Lions, where they saw the devastation of dead Zegrí, Gomel, and Maza knights who had died at the hands of the Abencerrajes, Gazules, and Alabeces. To this, Muza said, "If treason was done to the Abencerraje knights, it has been well avenged, although treason can never be truly compensated or satisfied."

His heart heavy from the sight, he headed to the Queen's chamber. They found her tearful and confused, accompanied by all her ladies-in-waiting. Among them was the beautiful Zelima, whom Muza loved greatly. Trembling, the Queen said to Muza, "What is this, Muza, my friend? What misfortune is this that resounds through the city and in the Alhambra for I cannot think what it is?"

Muza answered, "This is the King's business, for without due regard he agreed to a great betrayal of the Abencerraje knights, from whom he has received great and remarkable services. And in return, he has had thirty knights killed today, and there are even more inside in the Court of the Lions. This is the good work that the King my brother and your husband has carried out or allowed to be carried out today, and for which he has lost the kingdom. He may lose his life, too, if he appears, for all the people of Granada, both knights and the other estates, have taken my father Muley Hacén as their lord and king. This, my lady, is the cause of the commotion and riot that you hear."

NOTES

1 The Alijares was a royal palace on a small hill facing the much larger royal palace of the Alhambra.

2 The Generalife was a palace and garden complex constructed in the fourteenth century next to the older Alhambra palace and fortress, both situated atop a high hill above the city of Granada. The episode in question involved the one-on-one combat between a famed Christian knight and the King's half-brother, Muza.

3 The *juego de la sortija* is one of the many elaborate equestrian chivalric games that Pérez de Hita attributes to the Nasrid court, and involved spearing a ring with a lance from a galloping horse. Pérez de Hita also describes a number of elaborate floats to accompany the equestrian games. The Abencerrajes' motto echoes those of the Emperor Charles V, "Plus ultra" (ever further), and of his son Philip II of Spain, "Non sufficit orbis" (the world is not enough).

4 The Vega was the fertile plain outside the city of Granada, on which the city depended for food. These "heads" might refer to Christian captives who would later be sold back to the Christians for a sizable ransom or to cattle captured in raids.

5 Unlike "The Abencerraje," which never suggests that Abindarráez has any particular affinity for Christianity, Pérez de Hita develops sympathy for the Abencerrajes by making them friends to Christians and potential converts to Christianity, even as they are still fighting Christians and taking them captive.

Edicts and Official Documents
Concerning the Moriscos

The following documents trace the legal treatment of Muslims and Moriscos from the aftermath of the fall of Granada in 1492 to their expulsion in 1609 to 1614. They provide an important context for the novellas in this volume, as they suggest the strength of anti-Muslim and anti-Morisco animus, against which the texts offer their idealized protagonists.

The Christians violated the terms of the Nasrid surrender of Granada almost immediately, and a long period of increasing repression ensued, during which the authorities targeted not just Islam but a wide range of practices perceived to be "Moorish." Even in the brief period when, under Archbishop Hernando de Talavera, the official policy privileged syncretism and benign assimilation, there is no question that the population of Granada was being forced to abandon Islam ("Notice for the Inhabitants of the Albaicín" below). A number of the edicts, particularly the early ones, address only one town or one community, as in the very interesting treaty for Baza ("Agreement by Which the Moors of the Moorish Quarter of Baza and the Towns and Surrounding Areas Shall Convert to Catholicism"), giving a sense of the patchwork of control that was the most the Crown could hope for in the early years. Similarly, several edicts repeat previous legislation, indicating that earlier laws were not followed and were perhaps unenforceable. The frequent legislation against "Moorish" dress emphasizes the importance of visible signs of difference; paradoxically, one edict forbids Old Christian women from wearing "Moorish" cloaks, suggesting the wider circulation of the cultural forms the Crown attempted to connect to the Moriscos.

The most comprehensive and fully repressive body of laws is contained in the 1526 edict below. The Moriscos were successful in postponing the enforcement of these laws for over forty years, primarily through payments to the Crown. When the enforcement of the 1526 laws was finally announced in 1566–67, it led directly to the major Morisco uprising in the Alpujarras, which took the Crown over two years to subdue. (The petition by Francisco Núñez Muley, from which we also offer selections in this volume, was a last-ditch attempt by a Morisco notable to challenge the legislation.) In the wake of the uprising, Granadan Moriscos were exiled and forcibly relocated all over Spain; even this repression, however, failed to reassure the Crown of their loyalty. By the 1580s and 1590s, the debate about the possibility of assimilation had become radicalized, and many began calling for the Moriscos' expulsion from Spain, as evinced in the "Letter of Inquisitor-General Quiroga" below. The final outcome of this century of failed policies and increasing repression was the expulsion of the Moriscos—Christian subjects, who in some cases had been at least nominally Christian for generations—from the Peninsula, in 1609 to 1614, beginning with the Moriscos of the kingdom of Valencia ("Edict of Expulsion of the Moriscos of Valencia").

Notice for the Inhabitants of the Albaicín

(Exact date unknown, between 1497 and 1499)

Attributed to Fray Hernando de Talavera, Archbishop of Granada (1493–1507)[1]

Beloveds of Our Lord, good people, inhabitants of the Albaicín:

We received your petition and were very pleased to see your concern to learn and do what good Christians must. . . . So that you may all have full notice and a reminder of what we have told you at various times, we have put into writing here the sum total of rules that we want you to follow:

First, you must forget all ceremonies and anything Moorish in your prayers, fasts, celebrations, festivals, births, weddings, baths, funerary customs, and in all other things.

You must all know and teach your wives and your children, big and small, how to cross oneself and enter a church, to receive holy water, to say the Paternoster, the Ave Maria, and the Credo, to worship Our Lord in the holy Mass, and to adore the holy cross and venerate holy images with due reverence.

You must make sure to confess and take Communion, and ensure that your wives and your households confess and take Communion.

You must make sure to have all infants baptized within eight days of birth, or sooner if necessary.

You must make sure to have them confirmed in the Church as soon as possible.

As soon as they become ill, let them receive the sacraments of penitence and Communion, and the extreme unction on their deathbed.[2]

Let them make a will and perform works of charity as Catholic Christians, and let them and you be buried in consecrated cemeteries near your churches, as are those who are Christian by birth.[3]

Let them be married by their clerics, and when they are married let them receive the blessings in the church that, among the Christians, are called *velaciones* [nuptial benedictions]. . . .

You must send your children to church to learn to read and sing, or at least to learn the aforementioned prayers.

Those of you who know how to read must have all the books of prayers and psalms in Arabic that you shall be given, and all the ones mentioned in this notice, and you must follow them to pray in church. . . .

You must keep in your homes, in honest and clean places, some images of Our Lord or of the holy cross or of Our Lady the Virgin Mary, or of some saint; and beside that image you must keep the holy candle that will be blessed for you on the day of Our Lady, known as Saint Mary of the Candles.[4] And on the other side you must keep the holy palm that will be blessed for you on Palm Sunday. All of this pertains to the service of God, our Lord, and to the correct observance of our holy Catholic faith.

Moreover, so that your interactions do not incite scandal in those who are Christian by birth, and so that they do not think that you still follow the sect of Mohammed in your hearts, you must conform in all things and completely to the good and honest ways of good and honest

Christians: your dress, your shoes, your cosmetics, should be that of Christians; your diet, your table settings, and your meat should be prepared in the Christian manner. The way you walk, the way you give and take, the way you drink, and especially the way you speak should conform to the ways of Christians, forgetting as far as possible the Arabic language and ensuring that it is forgotten and never again spoken in your households.[5]

In order for certain persons to follow the aforementioned norms, it will be necessary to exert some pressure, and because the excommunication that we might perform is very dangerous and yet not feared by them. Therefore you and we both must beg the King and Queen, our lords, to set punishments for those who do not follow the norms and to ensure that these are carried out.

Agreement by Which the Moors of the Moorish Quarter of Baza and the Towns and Surrounding Areas Shall Convert to Catholicism

(30 September 1500)

King Ferdinand II and Queen Isabella I[6]

Because certain representatives of the Moors of the Moorish quarter of Baza and its towns and surrounding areas have notified us that said Moors will convert to our holy Catholic faith if we order relief from and suspension of some of the royal taxes collected from them in the city and in the towns and surrounding areas, and because we know how much this would serve and praise Our Lord and exalt and magnify our holy faith, we have decided to grant not only the favor of pardoning these taxes and royal rents now and forever, but also other reprieves and favors as outlined below:

First, we demand and it is our wish and our mercy that all of the said Moors, male and female, of the city of Baza and its surrounding towns and areas who have converted or shall convert to our holy Catholic faith, shall be free, absolved, and exempt from paying any of the Moorish dues[7] that they owe from the day they convert onward and forever. By this agreement, we free and exempt all those who have converted or who shall convert to our holy Catholic faith, as we have said, from paying taxes on their houses, farms, and all their property and lands, from the day they convert onward, and also their descendants from the said Moorish dues, as long as those who convert pay, from the day they convert onward and forever, the duties and harvest taxes that Christians pay on their work, harvests, livestock, and other things, just as the Christians do, and pay duties on all things that they sell and purchase according to the laws of our sales taxes. . . .

Moreover, all their receipts, contracts, and marriage agreements in Arabic signed by their *alfaquíes*[8] and *cadís*[9] shall continue to be enforced and observed henceforth as though they were issued by our own public notaries. . . .

Moreover, if any of them wish to go live in any other part of our kingdoms or territories where Christians live, they shall do so with absolutely no impediments. . . .

Moreover, our justices will punish in full anyone who calls them names such as "Moor" or "turn-coat." . . .

Moreover, when they take their children to church to show and teach them the things of our holy Catholic faith, they shall be treated as other Christians. . . .

Moreover, they shall not be pressured to buy and wear new clothes until the ones now worn by them and their wives need replacing.

⊞   Edict Ordering That Henceforth None   ⊞
of the Newly Converted in the Kingdom of Granada
Shall Make Themselves Clothing in the Moorish Fashion,
but Rather Shall Adopt the Style of Old Christians

(20 June 1511)

Doña Juana, on behalf of her father King Ferdinand II[10]

When the newly converted of this Kingdom of Granada converted to our holy Catholic faith, the majority of them agreed by mandate of the King, my lord and father, and the Queen, my lady mother (may she rest in holy glory), that from that moment on they would not recall the ways of the Moors, but instead act and live as Christians, for such they were. They were not to make any new Moorish clothing nor wear any beyond that which was already made, opting instead for the manner and fashion of Old Christians.

Now I have been informed that, despite the aforementioned [agreements], since that time the said newly converted, both men and women, have made and continue to make Moorish clothing and wear it in the fashion and manner worn in the time of the Moors.

Given that this was agreed upon and mandated, as we have mentioned above, we might prosecute those who contravened it. Yet because of the great desire the King, my lord and father, and I have to ensure that [the newly converted of this kingdom] be treated well in all things, having discussed this matter with some of the members of our Council and other persons, and with some of the newly converted of this kingdom in particular, it was agreed that I should send this letter with the following order. By which, and by any copy certified by a public notary, I firmly prohibit that from now on any of the newly converted of this kingdom, whether men or women, young or old, make for themselves or have made for them clothing in the fashion of the Moors. I order instead that they make clothing in the fashion of Old Christians. No tailor for any reason may sew or cut clothing for the newly converted that is not in the fashion of Old Christians. Any person who violates these rules will have that clothing confiscated, and any tailor who is found to have cut or sewn said clothing will incur a fine of two thousand *maravedís* payable to our treasury and will no longer be able to perform that occupation, but instead will be barred from it. With these punishments I condemn them from this moment on, without any further sentencing or declaration.

⊠ Edict Ordering Old Christian Women Not to Dress ⊠ in the Moorish Fashion or Wear *Almalafas*

(29 July 1513)

Secretary of Doña Juana, on behalf of her father King Ferdinand II[11]

I have been informed that some Old Christian women who live and reside in the city of Granada and other cities, towns, and areas of said kingdom dress in the Moorish fashion and cover themselves with *almalafas*,[12] ignoring our orders that the newly converted should leave behind Moorish clothing to dress in the fashion of Christians. Beyond the bad example that they give the newly converted, these [Old Christian] women, because they think that they are thus hidden and anonymous, participate in excesses and bad customs that do a disservice to Our Lord, bring dishonor upon themselves, and cause much harm.

Because it is my duty as Queen to address this matter, having consulted the King, my lord and father, and certain members of my Council, it was agreed that this letter of mine with the following order should be issued. By which, and by any copy certified by a public notary, I strongly forbid that henceforth any Old Christian woman dress in the Moorish fashion, under penalty that upon first offense she lose the clothing that she wears in this fashion and be given one hundred lashes, and upon second offense she suffer the same penalty and also be permanently exiled from the entire Kingdom of Granada. I order these punishments to go into effect immediately, without any further sentencing or declaration.

⊠   Edict Mandating What Should Be Done   ⊠
in the Kingdom of Granada in Light
of the Recent Inspections and
What Was Agreed in the Congregation
Celebrated in the Royal Chapel

(7 December 1526)

The Emperor, King Charles V[13]

Because kings should take great care to exalt our holy Catholic faith and thus extirpate, remove, and eradicate the errors of Christians, we will follow this obligation of ours, seeking to do everything in our power to fulfill our duty, so that we shall have less to answer for to God Our Lord. When I, the King, with my court, visited this great renowned city of Granada, we were notified that the newly converted there and in the other cities, towns, and provinces of its archbishopric had committed and have been committing every day many grave wrongs against our holy Catholic faith, observing their damned original sect of Mohammed and its errors and ceremonies despite having received the baptismal water of the Holy Spirit. We received several notices and petitions regarding these problems, and in order to punish what has occurred and remedy what is to come, having discussed the matter with the president and others on our council, and in consultation with me, we ordered the appointment of men of learning and conscience to visit and inspect the archbishopric in our name, for we are patrons of the churches of this Archbishopric of Granada. With the power of the dean and the chapter of the holy Church in this archbishopric, *sede vacante*,[14] they were to inquire after the things and cases in which the newly converted Moors in the archbishopric continue to follow the damned sect of Mohammed and its errors and ceremonies. Furthermore, so as not to give the newly converted reason or cause to persevere in their errors by claiming that the clerics who were supposed to teach them and the justices in that region committed crimes and other improprieties against them, I ordered [these men of learning and conscience] also to inform themselves about these issues so that I might address them and punish any wrongdoers. . . . The inspectors spread themselves throughout the archbishopric and personally performed their duty by interviewing many witnesses and bringing us information. Then, due to the great significance of this issue, and because its remedy would do such great service to God Our Lord and be so important for our holy Catholic faith, and because it is so worthy of remedy, we ordered a Congregation on the matter to bring together certain prelates residing in our court and members of the Royal Council of Castile and the Council of the Holy Inquisition on the matter. . . . Having considered the oral and written opinions that everyone offered, decided on, and declared regarding the matter, . . . they voted based on the authority of Holy Scripture and other principles of canon and civil law. They were all in agreement and of one vote, will, and opinion, with complete conformity. Once they had consulted with me, the King, it was agreed that to remedy the situation henceforth the following norms would be issued and executed:

First, because, as is well known, the Inquisition in these kingdoms serves God Our Lord and exalts our holy Catholic faith, henceforth in the city and archbishopric of Granada and in all the other cities, towns, and surrounding areas of this kingdom of Granada men of learning, conscience, and authority shall be appointed to administer the holy office of the Inquisition in these areas. . . . We earnestly charge these men with the task of caring for all matters concerning the souls of the newly converted Moors of this kingdom. . . .

In addition, the better to provide for this and in order to avoid any inconveniences and harm and to ensure that the bad things and harm that have occurred thus far in this kingdom shall no longer occur . . . we have approved and order that the following norms be issued and obeyed:

. . . This order decrees once more that none of the newly converted shall hold Moorish slaves in their houses or estates. We order that this rule be enforced. And because some might try to Christianize them in order to keep them, we order that they not keep as slaves any Christians, whether black or white, and that they not keep other Old Christian boys younger than 15 years in their service. Nor should they raise orphans or children of Old Christians, because of the harm it might cause.

Next, to avoid and remedy the harm and inconveniences that follow from the continued use of Arabic by the newly converted, we order that none of them, their children or any one of them shall henceforth speak in Arabic, nor shall there be any writing in Arabic. Everyone must speak Castilian. We also order that those who buy and sell and make contracts, whether inside or outside the silk market, shall not ask for anything or inquire about a price nor converse while buying or selling in Arabic, but rather in Castilian. The punishment, for the first offense, is three days in jail, and for the second offense, double the first. . . .

Furthermore, we order that neither the newly converted nor their sons or daughters, nor any one of them shall wear around their neck nor on any other place the pendants they usually wear that are inscribed with a hand and some Arabic letters.[15] No silversmith shall work on or make any of these or other pieces engraved or marked with moons or other Moorish letters and insignias, such as the Moors used to wear.[16] In their place, they shall wear crosses and other images. And the medallions and other pieces of jewelry that exist already, if they have all or any of the aforementioned markings, shall be melted and made into something else. . . .

Because the newly converted have ancient documents written in Arabic pertaining to their real estate and property, as well as other things, we order that these all be brought forth and presented, and that trustworthy people literate in that language translate them from Arabic into Castilian so that the parties who need a copy shall have one. And those that were written in Arabic shall be burned and torn so that there shall henceforth be absolutely no more writings in Arabic.

Great harm, inconvenience, and bad examples have resulted from those who frequent the baths in this kingdom. In order to stop these problems, and to prevent them from occurring in the future, we order that henceforth those who work in said baths be Old Christians, . . . and that none of the newly converted, neither men nor women, serve in these baths or hold a position there, under penalty of ten days in jail.

Moreover, it is highly inappropriate for newly converted women to wear *almalafas* and cover their faces. We order that henceforth none of them nor their children of any age shall wear *almafalas* or cloaks. If they want to wear them, they shall dye them any color they wish and keep their faces uncovered. And so that there be no deceit regarding this point, Old Christian women shall not cover their faces with a hat or a veil, but rather must keep their faces uncovered, even if they wear a hat. If this rule is not obeyed, our justices will confiscate the *almalafa* or cloak with which they are covered. . . . To best ensure this is followed and obeyed, we order and command that henceforth no more *almalafas* be made.

Furthermore, we henceforth forbid any women newly converted from Moors or any other person from painting their hands or feet or anything else with henna, whether publicly or in private.

Also, we henceforth forbid any *gazí*[17] who has been or is a captive or has been redeemed from living, residing, or traveling through the Alpujarras or along the sea coast or ten leagues beyond it, under penalty of imprisonment, for we have been informed that they are spies for the Moors and can cause other harm.

Furthermore, we order that henceforth no surgeon or doctor nor any other person shall allow the newly converted of this kingdom . . . to

cut the foreskin of the male member, without express license of a prelate or a governing official. Nor should they cut it themselves, and if this
is done without license, they shall forfeit all possessions and be exiled
permanently from the kingdom.

Moreover, we have been informed that some of the newly converted
people have redeemed Moors who are captive in these kingdoms [of
Spain] and sent them over to the other side [to North Africa],[18] and
they have many tactics and strategies to do this. We order that henceforth none of the newly converted shall redeem any Moor who does
not first convert to Christianity. And, once they have redeemed him,
they shall not keep him with them but rather shall place him in service
with some Old Christian person in order to teach him to live properly,
under penalty of three months of public prison in iron chains.

Moreover, although it is forbidden for the newly converted Moors
of this kingdom to have or bear arms, we have been informed that some
of them have license to bear them. We order that all those who have
these licenses shall bring the originals and present them to the mag-
istrates of said kingdom pertaining to their jurisdiction within thirty
days so that they may determine who should carry them and inform us
of what needs to be done. And until then, no one should carry them.
No landowners in this kingdom should harbor any murderers or crimi-
nals, or give license to any Morisco, even if he be their vassal, to bear
arms in any way. . . .

Moreover, we know that on some estates in this kingdom the owners take bribes and payoffs from those newly converted from Moors
in exchange for letting them keep some Moorish custom. We forbid
this and order that henceforth nothing of the sort be allowed, under
penalty that the owners of estates where this is done and allowed,
shall lose their jurisdiction, and forfeit it to the Royal Crown. And
because we want to know what has taken place until this point and
where it has occurred, we order our Council to investigate the matter
and bring the information before us, so that once we have examined
it, we may rule on it and remedy this issue immediately, as the case
requires.

Furthermore, the better to carry out what we mandate through
these laws, as well as for other reasons, until further notice those newly

converted from Moors in this kingdom shall not move from one town to the other, under penalty of exile, at our discretion.

Furthermore, we order that the authorities of the cities, towns, and provinces of this kingdom shall live in their respective jurisdictions, because we are informed that some jurisdictions have no Old Christians living in them.

Furthermore, we have been informed that the newly converted will not eat meat if it is not butchered by the hand of one who is circumcised. Because this is an evil deed, which we shall not allow or suffer to be performed in any fashion, but rather prohibit and proscribe so that they do not persevere in their rites and things of the damned original sect of Mohammed, therefore, we order that henceforth, where there is an Old Christian who can butcher meat, none of the newly converted from Moors may butcher meat. And if there is no Old Christian available who is able or willing to butcher the meat, we command that a person of the clergy from that region approve someone else to do it, accepting nothing in exchange for the approval. . . .

Furthermore, because we have been informed that newly converted people frequently marry with special dispensations, some of which concern things that are strongly forbidden, we will write to His Holiness to issue a Bull so that the newly converted may not be married with dispensations unless they have been seen and approved by a prelate, who shall personally examine the justification for the dispensation. . . .

Moreover, we have been informed that some of the newly converted use Moorish names and last names. We order that henceforth they shall not use them, and that if any of them currently has a Moorish name or last name, he should get rid of it and no longer use it and take a Christian name instead. Furthermore, we order that they shall not call each other "dogs" or "Moors" and that no one else shall call them those names publicly or in private, and if anyone of the newly converted contravenes anything in this chapter, he must spend ten days in jail, and if any Old Christian does so, he must spend six; and we order our justices to obey and follow this order, and that upon the second offence the sentence be doubled.

⬛ Edict Ordering the Newly Converted ⬛
to Change Their Dress

(1 July 1530)

Queen Isabella[19]

Honest newly converted vassals of our Kingdom of Granada:

You already know that the Emperor and King, my husband, during his visit to the city [of Granada], motivated by saintly zeal and purpose, ordered certain rules to be followed and observed for your salvation. One of the principal things that you are to follow and help with, God's grace permitting, is to remove things that give you occasion to remember the bad sect [of Islam] and the past errors in which you used to live. This is principally the case with the habits and dress that you wear from when you were not Christians, and therefore, to serve God and Us, we order and plead you that you leave behind said habit and henceforth that you and your children dress and wear clothing and habits in the fashion of Old Christians in that kingdom. Because, beyond benefiting the remedy and salvation of your souls, you would please me and serve me very much by doing so, and I will always remember it and grant you favors for it. Because I am sending the reverend father archbishop of Granada of our Council to speak to you more at length on my behalf about this issue, I ask you to listen to, credit, and believe what he tells you.

⬛ Edict Regarding the Music, Songs, ⬛
and Dances of the Newly Converted

(10 March 1532)

Queen Isabella[20]

President and judges of our Court and Chancery who reside in the city of Granada:

On behalf of the New Christians of the Kingdom of Granada, I have been informed that we recently ordered them not to play music, sing, or dance, or make any such kind of celebration, not even for their wedding festivities. This is because certain songs named Mohammed and because the *gazís* and *harbis*,[21] who are slaves and captives, danced certain *zambras*[22] full of dishonesty and bad things, which, had good and honest people heard of it, would have greatly vexed them. They requested me to punish those who sing songs of Mohammed and other songs we have forbidden, and to forbid the said captive slaves and free people from celebrating in such ways or gathering to do so. The rest, they requested, should be given license to play music, sing, and dance with their musical instruments in their weddings and pastimes, as they have done since becoming Christians, leaving this up to my discretion.

Therefore, I command you to review the edict issued on these matters when the Emperor, my husband, was in that city, and what was instructed according to his mandate. May you carry out what you believe most convenient regarding the aforementioned issues.

⊠ Letter of Inquisitor-General Quiroga ⊠
Suggesting the Expulsion of the Moriscos

(7 May 1590)[23]

Most reverend Inquisitors:

Considering the multitude of new converts from Moorishness in these kingdoms of Castile and in all its towns and in those of the Crown of Aragon and how it grows day by day, and how mixed they are among the Catholic Christians and how acculturated[24] and well informed of their things, and that their way of life and profession of Christianity shows little fruit and allows no hope for any, and that they are such enemies of ours, as we have seen and see and as everyday experience shows, we must take care to look into it and inform ourselves— for even His Majesty desires this—whether it is convenient for these to be among us as they are at present, or whether it would be good to order and cause them to be separated and removed, depriving them of the opportunity that one may well expect of them if they ever perceive it, God forbid, to unsettle these kingdoms and disturb them. And if this were approved, how would it be ordered and what should be done with them and where and in what parts should they be placed so as to be secure, so that this business should be achieved with due consideration to its import and gravity, considering the reasons that might argue for and against it and informing us of them punctually and in detail and as soon as possible. May God keep your reverend persons.

❖ Edict of Expulsion of the Moriscos of Valencia ❖

(22 September 1609)

Philip III[25]

Marquis of Carazena, my cousin, liuetenant and Captain General of my kingdom of Valencia:

You all know how over the course of so many years I have sought the conversion of the Moriscos of this kingdom [Valencia] and of Castile, how they were granted edicts of grace, how we have strived to instruct them in our holy faith, and how little it has served. For we have seen none of them convert, but rather their obstinacy grow. And for I was aware of the danger, and the irredeemable harm that could come from their dissimulation, many very learned and holy men came to me several days ago, begging me to apply the quick remedy that my conscience required in order to placate our Lord, who is so offended by these people. They assured me that I could, without any scruples, punish them by taking their lives and property, for their perseverance in their crimes convicted them of heresy, apostasy, and treason against divine and human majesty. Although I might have punished them with the rigor that their faults deserved, I still hoped to change their minds by soft and gentle means, and so convened the council which you, the Patriarch, and other prelates and learned persons attended, to inquire whether it might be justified to remove them from these kingdoms. It being known that those from [the kingdom of Valencia] and from Castile persisted in their harmful intent, I received reliable reports that, continuing their apostasy and treason, they have sought and still seek to harm and disturb our kingdoms through their ambassadors and other means. I wish to fulfill my duties to secure the conservation and safety of our kingdoms, and in particular that of Valencia and its good and faithful subjects, whose danger is most evident, and to end this heresy and apostasy. So, after putting matters in the hands of our Lord, and trusting in His divine favor where His honor and glory are concerned, I have decided to expel all the Moriscos from this kingdom and to cast them upon Barbary.

And so that this be executed and what His Majesty orders be correctly enacted, we have ordered the publication of the following decree:

1. First, within three days of the publication of this decree in the places where each Morisco resides and has a house, all the Moriscos of this kingdom, men as well as women, with their children, must leave and embark ship where the commissioner responsible orders them to, obeying him and his orders. They must take with them what belongings they can carry and embark on the galleys and ships that are ready to take them to Barbary, where they will be disembarked with no mistreatment or harm to their persons or their belongings, physical or verbal. They are to be provided with any food necessary to sustain them during their embarkation, and they must also carry what food they can. Anyone who does not comply or exceeds in any way what is contained in this decree will incur the penalty of death, which will be peremptorily enacted.

2. Three days after the publication of this decree and until the first embarkation, any Morisco found outside of custody or the place where he should be, traveling along the roads or other places, may be arrested by anyone. This person may, without punishment, seize [the Morisco]'s belongings and turn him in to the nearest authorities; and if [the Morisco] defends himself, he may kill him.

3. Under the same penalty, once this decree has been published no Moriscos may leave their places of residence for any other, but must not move until the commissioner who will take them to the embarkation comes for them.

4. Should any Morisco hide or bury any belongings, in order not to take them with him, or set fire to them or to his houses, fields, gardens, or orchards, all those who reside in that place will incur the penalty of death. . . .

6. No Old Christian or soldier, whether a native of this kingdom or not, shall dare to mistreat said Moriscos, their wives, children or any of theirs by words or deeds, or attempt to take their belongings. . . .

7. Nor may anyone hide [Moriscos] in their houses, harboring them or helping them, under penalty of six years in the galleys. . . .

8. So that the Moriscos may understand that His Majesty's intention is only to expel them from his kingdoms, that they will not be harmed in the voyage, and that they will be set ashore on the Barbary coast, we authorize ten of the said Moriscos who embark on the first voyage to return in order to inform the others. And the same shall be done on every subsequent voyage. . . .

9. Children under four years of age who wish to stay shall not be expelled, as long as their parents or guardians (should they be orphans) agree.

10. Children under six years of age whose father is an Old Christian shall stay, and their mother with them, even is she is a Morisca. But if the father is a Morisco and she is an Old Christian, he shall be expelled, and the children under six shall remain with the mother.

11. The same shall apply to those who have lived among Christians for a period such as two years, without attending the councils of the community [alhama].

12. The same shall apply to those who receive the Holy Sacrament with permission from their prelates, as attested by the rectors of the places where they live.

13. His Majesty approves any of the said Moriscos moving to other kingdoms if they so desire, as long as they do not pass through those of Spain and leave for them from their places of residence within the allotted time.

NOTES

1 Excerpted from Archivo de Simancas, *Diversos de Castilla*, leg. 8, f. 114, as transcribed in Antonio Gallego Burín and Alfonso Gámir Sandoval, *Los moriscos del reino de Granada, según el sínodo de Guadix de 1554* (1996), 161–63.

2 The author has been using the second person to address his audience and the third person to describe the children whom the heads of households must have baptized and confirmed. Here, the entire recommendation concerns those third-person children, almost as though acknowledging via grammar that true assimilation will occur not for the first generation of converts but for those brought up in a new religious practice.

3 The original has *cristianos de nación*—Christians by birth, or of the Christian nation—an interesting analogy with the distinction between "turcos de nación" and "turcos

de profesión"—Turks by birth versus professed Turks—used to describe Muslims and renegades in North Africa, the Ottoman Empire, and across the Mediterranean world.

4 The ceremony referred to is Candlemas, also known as the Presentation of Jesus at the Temple or the Purification of the Virgin—with interesting connotations of participation in rites that do not fit precisely, given that Mary, as a virgin, did not require ritual purification. The Virgin of Candelaria was associated with the conversion of the Guanche people in the Canary Islands after the Spanish conquest in the fifteenth century, and was represented as dark skinned.

5 This commmand to "forget Arabic" appears soon after mentioning that manuals of Christian prayers in Arabic shall be distributed among new converts who know how to read, demonstrating the contradictions and difficulties the Crown encountered in its attempt to teach Christianity in meaningful terms to new converts while also eradicating cultural forms that would remind them of their non-Christian past. Questions of language and translation for correct evangelization would be hotly debated throughout the expanding Spanish Empire in the sixteenth century.

6 Excerpted from Archivo del Ayuntamiento de Baza, *Provisiones antiguas*, 1497–1508, as transcribed in Gallego Burín and Gámir Sandoval, 163–66.

7 "Moorish dues" (*derechos moriscos*) were taxes charged by Islamic law, which the Catholic Monarchs had been collecting even after replacing Muslim rule in southern Spain. When a papal bull from March 22, 1500, limited the Spanish Crown to the right to keep only two thirds of these "Moorish dues," granting the other third to the Church, it began to offer as incentive for Muslims to convert the waiving of the previous tax system for that of Old Christians (Harvey 2005, 46).

8 Scholars specializing in Muslim law.

9 Judges of Muslim law.

10 Excerpted from Archivo del Ayuntamiento de Granada, *Indiferentes*, leg. 2003, as transcribed in Gallego Burín and Gámir Sandoval, 174–75.

Juana (1479–1555) inherited the throne of Castile after the death of her mother Isabella but reigned only for a short time due to her supposed mental instability. Her father, Ferdinand II, was named regent in her stead until his death in 1516.

11 Archivo del Ayuntamiento de Granada, *Libro 6 de Proviciones*, f. 308, as transcribed in Gallego Burín and Gámir Sandoval, 179–80.

12 Moorish cloaks.

13 Excerpted from Archivo de la Iglesia Catedral de Granada, *Reales Cédulas*, lib. II duplicado, f. 70, as transcribed in Gallego Burín and Gámir Sandoval, 198–205.

14 "The seat being empty": This Latin expression from canon law refers to a vacancy in an episcopal see.

15 The "hand of Fatima," also known as Hamsa, is an upright hand worn in Muslim, Jewish, and eastern Christian traditions to protect the wearer from evil.

16 The crescent moon often symbolized Islamic political power and was frequently displayed on the flags of Muslim rulers in the Middle East and North Africa during this period.

17 A Muslim from North Africa who has converted to Christianity, or his or her descendants.

18 The expression *allende* was commonly used for North Africa.

19 Archivo de la Iglesia Catedra de Granada, *Reales Cédulas*, lib. II duplicado, f. 11, as transcribed in Gallego Burín and Gámir Sandoval, 220.

Isabella of Portugal (1503–39) was married to Charles V in 1526 and served as regent of Spain during her husband's lengthy absences, hence the edict in her name.

20 *Cédulas, provisiones, visitas y ordenanzas de la Audiencia de Granada* [Granada, 1551], f. 102v, as transcribed in Gallego Burín and Gámir Sandoval, 234.

21 This term is probably a Spanish version of the Arabic term *harbī*, which means someone from *al-harb* (the realm of war and conflict). In this context, it probably refers to Muslims captured by Christians in war.

22 A Moorish dance.

23 Archivo Histórico Nacional, *Inquisición de Valencia, Cartas del Consejo*, Legajo 5, número 1, folio 254, as transcribed in Henry Charles Lea, *The Moriscos of Spain*, 438.

24 *Ladina* is the term used to describe Daraja in "Ozmín and Daraja" for her ability to speak Spanish with little or no marked accent.

25 Excerpted from Archivo General de Simancas, Estado, 2638bis, number 63, as reproduced in Manuel Danvila y Collado, *La expulsión de los moriscos españoles: Conferencias pronunciadas en el Ateneo de Madrid*, 344–47.

From "A Petition to the Court"

FRANCISCO NÚÑEZ MULEY

The Granadan Morisco Francisco Núñez Muley was probably born soon after the fall of the city to the Christian forces in 1492. He lived through various official stances toward religious difference, from the brief initial tolerance of Islam, to the forced baptisms of the turn of the sixteenth century, to the severely repressive royal ordinances against Moorish cultural practices as the century progressed. Núñez Muley was converted to Christianity as a child and served as a page in the household of the tolerant archbishop of Granada, Hernando de Talavera. His name appears in the records of several negotiations with the Crown on behalf of the Moriscos. Núñez Muley was thus a natural choice to petition Don Pedro de Deza, head of the Royal Audiencia and Chancery Court of Granada, against the 1566–67 decrees forbidding the Moriscos from using Arabic or engaging in traditional cultural practices. His 1567 petition was a last-minute attempt to hold back the tide of increasing repression, against which the Moriscos would eventually rebel in late 1568. Núñez Muley challenges the laws point by point. He recalls the initial terms on which Granada had surrendered, to underscore the Christian betrayal that underlies the Morisco "problem." He questions the prohibitions against "Moorish" dress by arguing that it is properly *Granadan*—that is, a sign of regional identity rather than of ethnic or religious difference. More broadly, he argues for the importance of Moorish forms within the history of Spain, questioning official attempts to erase the Arabic language and the histories associated with it.

The original *memorial* is in the Biblioteca Nacional in Madrid, Sección de Ms., 6176 (R.29), ff. 311–331 obverse. We have based our translation on the version edited by K. Garrad (1954) as "The Original Memorial of Don Francisco Núñez Muley." For a complete translation, see Francisco Núñez Muley, *A Memorandum for the President of the Royal Audiencia and Chancery Court of the City and Kingdom of Granada* (2007).

First of all, it is stated [in the decrees] that at the time when the natives of this kingdom converted to our holy Catholic faith, they agreed to change their dress and that their ancient memories should be lost. I think there is no memory by anyone in this kingdom of such a pact and agreement, which never existed, nor will it appear in writing, for the conversion of the natives of this kingdom was by force and against what had been granted by the Catholic Monarchs to Muley Boabdil,[1] who was the ruler of this kingdom, and his officials, and they all signed their names to it, on both sides, with more than forty articles to it. [The treaty] was drawn up and agreed upon at the time when the king and the city governors handed over this city and its kingdom. What was agreed to in these articles was that [the natives] would remain in their faith and continue as they used to do in their mosques and with their *alcaldes* [judges] and *almotís* [religious leaders] and *alfaquís* [scholars],[2] and receive the rents from the lands belonging to their mosques, and that they would not be converted into Christians, and other things that are spelled out in that treaty and its articles, which I have referred to.

And as to whether [traditional Morisco] dress and footwear continue in the ceremonies and customs of Muslims: in this, my lord, it seems to me from my own poor judgment and what I have learned from my fellow elders, that these reports are not complete or valid. For this dress and costume and footwear cannot be said to be Muslim, nor is it specific to Muslims. It may be said to be the costume of this kingdom and province—as in all the kingdoms of Castile and the other kingdoms and provinces they have costumes that differ from each other, and all of them Christian, so the said dress and costume of this kingdom is very different from the costume of the Muslims from the other side[3] and from the Barbary Coast; and there also are very great differences from one kingdom to the next—what they wear in Fez is not exactly what they wear in Estremeçen, and in Turkey it is completely different, and all of them are Muslim. So one cannot prove or say that the costume of the newly converted ones [in Granada] is Muslim costume;

nor can it be proved, for the Christians of the holy house of Jerusalem and all that Christian kingdom and its learned men, as they have been seen in this city, came in dress and headdress like those from the other side, and not in Castilian dress, and they are Christians. Nor do they know the Castilian tongue, and yet they are Catholic Christians. Hence, and as I have said, Christianity does not depend on the dress nor on the footwear that is worn now, nor does the Muslim sect.

With respect to Moorish surnames: how are people to know and deal with each other if they have only Christian surnames? Moorish persons and lineages shall be lost, and no one will know whom they deal with or buy from or marry if they do not know their original lineage. For what is the point of wanting to lose such remembrances, or the costume and dress, or the last names, or all that I have mentioned? Does not their preservation do great honor to the Kings who won these kingdoms, showing the diverse ways in which they won them? This was the Catholic Monarchs' intention in protecting this kingdom in the way that they did, as did previous archbishops; and this was the intention and will of the Emperors and Catholic Monarchs in protecting the memory of the royal houses of the Alhambra and other memories, so that they would remain as they had been in the time of the Moorish kings, in order that what their Highnesses had won should show and appear more clearly.

NOTES

1 Núñez Muley refers here to the Capitulaciones de Granada, the terms of surrender for Granada, negotiated between Ferdinand and Isabella, the Catholic Monarchs, and the last of the Nasrid kings, Abū 'Abd Allah, often referred to as the Small King or Boabdil.

2 We have retained Núñez Muley's terms here. It is interesting to ponder how familiar these words might have been to Spanish speakers by the 1560s.

3 The expression *moros de allende* was commonly used to describe Muslims in North Africa.

Bibliography

Selected First Editions in Spanish

Alemán, Mateo. *Primera parte de Guzmán de Alfarache*. Madrid: Casa del Licenciado Varez de Castro, 1599.

Historia del Abencerraje y la hermosa Jarifa. Toledo: Miguel Ferrer, 1561.

Historia del Abencerraje y la hermosa Jarifa. Edited by Antonio de Villegas. Medina del Campo: Franciso del Canto, 1565.

Historia del Abencerraje y la hermosa Jarifa. In undated *Historia del Moro* sixteenth-century manuscript.

Montemayor, Jorge de. *Diana*. Valladolid: Francisco Fernández de Córdoba, 1561.

Selected First-Edition Translations

Alemán, Mateo. *Guzman de Alfarache—vitae humanae proscenium*. Translated by Gaspar Ens. Cologne: Excudebat Petrus à Brachel, 1623.

———. *Het leven van Gusman d'Alfarache*. 2 parts. Rotterdam: A. Pietersz, 1655.

———. *Der Landtstörtzer: Gusman von Alfarche oder Picaro genannt: dessen wunderbarliches, abenthewelichs vnd possirlichs Leben . . . hierin beschriben wirdt*. Translated by Aegidius Albertinus. Munich: Henricus, 1615.

———. *The Rogue; or, the Life of Guzman de Alfarache: Written in Spanish by Matheo Aleman, Servant to His Catholike Maiestie, and Born in Sevil*. Translated by James Mabbe. London: Printed [by Eliot's Court Press and George Eld] for Edward Blount, 1623.

———. *Vita del picaro Gusmano d'Alfarace*. Translated by Barezzo Barezzi. Venice: Barezzo Barezzi, 1606.

Montemayor, Jorge de. *Diana of George of Montemayor: Translated Out of Spanish into English by Bartholomew Yong of the Middle Temple Gentleman*. London: Edm. Bollifant, impensis G[eorge] B[ishop], 1598.

———. *Les sept livres de la Diane*. Translated by Jean de Foigny. Rheims: Jean de Foigny, 1578.

Selected Modern Editions

El Abencerraje (novela y romancero). Edited by Francisco López Estrada. Madrid: Cátedra, 1996.

El Abencerraje y la hermosa Jarifa: Cuatro textos y su estudio. Edited by Francisco López Estrada. Madrid: Publicaciones de la Revista de Archivos, Bibliotecas y Museos, 1957.

Alemán, Mateo. *Guzmán de Alfarache*. 2 vols. Edited by José María Micó. Madrid: Cátedra, 1997.

———. *The Rogue; or, the Life of Guzman de Alfarache. Written in Spanish by Matheo Aleman and Done into English by James Mabbe*. Translated by James Mabbe. London: Constable, 1924.

Durán, Agustín, ed. *Romancero general*. Madrid: Rivadeneyra, 1851.

Montemayor, Jorge de, and Gil Polo. *A Critical Edition of Yong's Translation of George of Montemayor's "Diana" and Gil Polo's Enamoured Diana*. Edited by Judith M. Kennedy. Oxford: Clarendon, 1968.

Pérez de Hita, Ginés. *Guerras civiles de Granada*. 2 vols. Edited by Paula Blanchard-Demouge. Madrid: Bailly-Baillière, 1913.

Secondary Sources

Bass, Laura. "Homosocial Bonds and Desire in the Abencerraje." *Revista Canadiense de Estudios Hispánicos* 24.3 (Spring 2000): 453–71.

Bollard, Kathleen. "Re-reading heroism in El Abencerraje." *Bulletin of Spanish Studies* 80.3 (2003): 297–307.

Burshatin, Israel. "Power, Discourse, and Metaphor in the *Abencerraje*." *MLN* 99.2 (March 1984): 195–213.

Cantos Benítez, Pedro de. *Escrutinio de maravedises, y monedas de oro antiguas, su valor, reduccion, y cambio a las monedas corrientes: Deducido de escrituras, leyes, y pragmaticas antiguas, y modernas de España*. Madrid: Antonio Marín, 1763.

Carrasco Urgoiti, Maria Soledad. "La cuestión morisca reflejada en la narrativa del Siglo de Oro." In *Destierros argoneses (vol.1) Judíos y Moriscos*, 229–53. Zaragoza: Institución Fernando el Católico, 1988.

———. "Las cortes señoriales del Aragón mudéjar y *El Abencerraje*." In *Homenaje a Casalduero: crítica y poesía*, edited by Rizel Pincus Sigele and Gonzalo Sobejano, 115–28. Madrid: Gredos, 1972.

———. "La 'Historia de Ozmín y Daraja' de Mateo Alemán en la trayectoria de la novela morisca." In *Estudios sobre la novela breve de tema Morisco*, 105–26. Barcelona: Bellaterra, 2005.

———. *The Moorish Novel: "El Abencerraje" and Pérez de Hita*. Boston: Twayne, 1976.

Castro, Américo. *España en su historia: Cristianos, moros y judíos*. Buenos Aires: Losada, 1948.

Catlos, Brian A. "Contexto y conveniencia en la corona de Aragón: Propuesta de un modelo de interacción entre grupos etno-religiosos minoritarios y mayoritarios." *Revista d'Història Medieval* 12 (2001): 259–68.

Cavillac, Michel. "Ozmín y Daraja à l'épreuve de l'*Atalaya*." *Bulletin Hispanique* 92.1 (1990): 141–84.

Cervantes Saavedra, Miguel de. *Don Quixote*. Translated by Edith Grossman. New York: Harper Collins, 2003.

Cohen, Walter. "The Uniqueness of Spain." In *Echoes and Inscriptions: Comparative Approaches to Early Modern Spanish Literatures*, edited by Barbara A. Simerka and Christopher B. Weimer, 17–29. Lewisburg, Pa.: Bucknell University Press, 2000.

Coleman, David. *Creating Christian Granada: Society and Religious Culture in an Old-World Frontier City, 1492–1600*. Ithaca, N.Y.: Cornell University Press, 2003.

Covarrubias, Sebastián de. *Tesoro de la lengua castellana o española*. Madrid: Luis Sánchez, 1611.

Danvila y Collado, Manuel. *La expulsión de los moriscos españoles: Conferencias pronunciadas en el Ateneo de Madrid* [1889]. Edited by Rafael Benítez Sánchez-Blanco. Valencia: Universitat de Valencia, 2007.

Diccionario de la Real Academia Española. 22nd edition. 2001. Real Academia Española. 7 September 2013. http://www.rae.es/rae.html.

Dodds, Jerrilynn. "The Mudejar Tradition in Architecture." In *The Legacy of Muslim Spain* (2 vols.), edited by Salma Khadra Jayyusi, 2: 592–98. Leiden: Brill, 1994.

Dodds, Jerrilynn; María Rosa Menocal; and Abigail Krasner Balbale. *The Arts of Intimacy: Christians, Jews, and Muslims in the Making of Castilian Culture*. New Haven: Yale University Press, 2008.

Feliciano Chaves, María Judith. "*Mudejarismo* in Its Colonial Context: Iberian Cultural Display, Viceregal Luxury Consumption, and the Negotiation of Identities in Sixteenth-Century New Spain." Ph.D. diss., University of Pennsylvania, 2004.

———. "Muslim Shrouds for Christian Kings: A Reassessment of Andalusi Textiles in Thirteenth-Century Castilian Life and Ritual." In *Under the Influence: Questioning the Comparative in Medieval Castile*, edited by Cynthia Robinson and Leyla Rouhi, 101–31. Boston/Leiden: Brill, 2005.

Feliciano, María Judith, and Leyla Rouhi. "Introduction." In *Interrogating Iberian Frontiers*, edited by Barbara F. Weissberger, with guest editors Feliciano, Rouhi, and Cynthia Robinson. *Medieval Encounters* 12.3 (2006): 317–28.

Fuchs, Barbara. *Exotic Nation: Maurophilia and the Construction of Early Modern Spain*. Philadelphia: University of Pennsylvania Press, 2009.

———. *Mimesis and Empire: The New World, Islam, and European Identities*. Cambridge: Cambridge University Press, 2001.

———. *Passing for Spain: Cervantes and the Fictions of Identity*. Urbana: University of Illinois Press, 2003.

Gallego Burín, Antonio, and Alfonso Gámir Sandoval. *Los moriscos del reino de Granada, según el sínodo de Guadix de 1554*. Granada: Archivum, 1996.

Garrad, K. "The Original Memorial of Don Francisco Núñez Muley." *Atlante* 2 (1954): 199–226.

González Alcantud, José A. *Lo moro: Las lógicas de la derrota y la formación del estereotipo islámico*. Barcelona: Anthropos, 2002.

Greer, Margaret; Maureen Quilligan; and Walter Mignolo, eds. *Rereading the Black Legend: The Discourses of Religious and Racial Difference in the Renaissance Empires*. Chicago: University of Chicago Press, 2007.

Griffin, Eric. "From Ethos to Ethnos: Hispanizing 'the Spaniard' in the Old World and the New." *New Centennial Review* 2.1 (Spring 2002): 69–116.

Guillén, Claudio. "Literature as a Historical Contradiction: *El Abencerraje*, the Moorish Novel, and the Eclogue." In *Literature as System: Essays Toward the Theory of Literary History*. Princeton, N.J.: Princeton University Press, 1971.

Harris, A. Katie. *From Muslim to Christian Granada: Inventing a City's Past in Early Modern Spain*. Baltimore: Johns Hopkins University Press, 2007.

Harvey, L. P. *Islamic Spain, 1250–1500*. Chicago: University of Chicago Press, 1990.

———. *Muslims in Spain: 1500–1614*. Chicago: University of Chicago Press, 2005.

———. "The Political, Social, and Cultural History of the Moriscos." In *The Legacy of Muslim Spain* (2 vols.), edited by Salma Khadra Jayyusi, 1: 201–39. Leiden: Brill, 1994.

Hillgarth, J. N. *The Mirror of Spain, 1500–1700: The Formation of a Myth*. Ann Arbor: University of Michigan Press, 2003.

Holzinger, Walter. "The Militia of Love, War, and Virtue in the *Abencerraje y la hermosa Jarifa*: A Structural and Sociological Reassessment." *Revista Canadiense de Estudios Hispánicos* 2.3 (1978): 227–38.

Lea, Henry Charles. *The Moriscos of Spain*. Philadelphia: Lea Brothers, 1901.

Liss, Peggy K. *Isabel the Queen: Life and Times*. Philadelphia: University of Pennsylvania Press, 2004.

López Estrada, Francisco. "*El Abencerraje* de Toledo, 1561: Edición crítica y comentarios." *Anales de la Universidad Hispalense* 19 (1959): 1–60.

———. "Introducción." In *El Abencerraje* (novela y romancero), edited by Francisco López Estrada, 13–113. Madrid: Cátedra, 1996.

McGrady, Donald. "Heliodorus' Influence on Mateo Aleman." *Hispanic Review* 34.1 (Jan. 1966): 49–53.

Morell, Hortensia. "La deformación picaresca del mundo ideal en *Ozmín y Daraja del Guzmán de Alfarache*." *La Torre* 13.87–88 (1975): 101–25.

Muldoon, James. *Varieties of Religious Conversion in the Middle Ages*. Gainesville: University Press of Florida, 1997.

Nalle, Sara. "Printing and Reading Popular Texts Sixteenth-Century Spain." In *Culture and the State in Spain, 1550–1850*, edited by Thomas E. Lewis and Francisco J. Sánchez, 126–56. New York: Garland, 1999.

Núñez Muley, Francisco. *A Memorandum for the President of the Royal Audiencia and Chancery Court of the City and Kingdom of Granada*. Edited and translated by Vincent Barletta. Chicago: University of Chicago Press, 2007.

Root, Deborah. "Speaking Christian: Orthodoxy and Difference in Sixteenth-Century Spain." *Representations* 23 (1988): 118–34.

Shipley, George A. "La obra literaria como monumento histórico: El caso de *El Abencerraje*." *Journal of Hispanic Philology* 2.2 (Winter 1978): 118–19.

Tueller, James B. *Good and Faithful Christians: Moriscos and Catholicism in Early Modern Spain*. New Orleans: University Press of the South, 2002.

Valencia, Pedro de. *Tratado acerca de los moriscos de España* [1606]. Facsimile edition edited by Joaquín Gil Sanjuan. Málaga: Algazara, 1997.

Verdaguer Clavera, Isabel. "Problems in Translating Guzmán de Alfarache into English." *SEDERI: Journal of the Spanish Society for English Renaissance Studies* 4 (1993): 273–79.

Vigo Gutiérrez, Abelardo del. *Cambistas, mercaderes y banqueros en el Siglo de Oro español.* Madrid: Biblioteca de Autores Cristianos, 1997.

Vilches, Elvira. "Coins, Value, and Trust: The Problematics of *Vellón* in Seventeenth-Century Spanish Culture." In *Signs of Power in Habsburg Spain and the New World*, edited by Jason McCloskey and Ignacio López Alemany, 95–112. Lewisburg, Pa.: Bucknell University Press, 2013.

Weissberger, Barbara F. *Isabel Rules: Constructing Queenship, Wielding Power.* Minneapolis: University of Minnesota Press, 2004.

Whitenack, Judith A. "The *alma diferente* of Mateo Alemán's 'Ozmín y Daraja.'" *Romance Quarterly* 38.1 (1991): 59–71.

Yiacoup, Sizen. "Memory and Acculturation in the Late Medieval and Early Modern Frontier Ballad." *Journal of Romance Studies* 4.3 (Winter 2004): 61–78.

Acknowledgments

We are grateful to our colleagues Elvira Vilches, Javier Irigoyen-García, and Vincent Barletta, who answered our queries and questions throughout the composition of these translations with invaluable insight and expertise.